Mackinac Passage: Pirate Party

Robert A.

Illustrated by
Bill Williams

EDCO Publishing, Inc.
2648 Lapeer Rd.
Auburn Hills, MI 48326
www.edcopublishing.com

Printed in the United States of America

ISBN-10: 0-9749412-5-5
ISBN-13: 978-0-9749412-5-7
Library of Congress Control Number: 2005929246

ACKNOWLEDGEMENTS

I write these stories for fun, but the fun comes not from the thousands of hours spent hunched over a computer or poring through stacks of books in a small room at odd hours of the day and night. The real joy stems from the people I meet while researching the books' topics and the many more after publication who relate associated tales of their own. As with each of my other stories, I have many people to acknowledge for this book's publication. The brief recognition given in this space is hardly a beginning for the appreciation and affection I have for their efforts. They are:

Phil Porter, Chief Curator Mackinac Island State Historic Parks and club organizer/star/mid-field scout of the Mackinac Island Never Sweats.

Gloria Whelan, author of many award-winning books and friend.

Nancy Bujold, assistant director, Capital Area District Library.

Andy Maas, fellow Granger, reader of an early draft and fine young man.

Margaret Doud, Mayor of Mackinac Island and proprietor of the first-class Windermere Hotel.

Jeff Hancks, public service librarian of the Clarke Library at CMU.

Walker Lytle, grandson, expert critic and fish catcher.

Candy Lee, teacher, editor and friend.

Linda McGarry, teacher, editor and friend.

Javan Kienzle, author, constant supporter, editor and friend.

Ken Johnson, sharp-eyed neighbor, fellow Rotarian and former racquetball partner.

Bert Schafer, newly found acquaintance and fellow lover of Great Lakes nautical lore.

Bill Williams, award-winning artist and illustrator.

PROLOGUE

My name is Will Drake. I am 15 years old and have lived all my life in New York City, a grand town of some 10,000 people. My father has just taken a job with a new fur-trading company, owned by a man called John Jacob Astor. I have said goodbye to my schoolmates, neighbors and, most importantly, a settled and civilized life on the East Coast of the United States of America.

With our possessions crammed into an oxcart, my parents and I have crossed westward overland to Buffalo, a small village on the eastern shore of Lake Erie. There we boarded the four-masted passenger schooner *Ticonderoga*.

We are now sailing toward our new home in Michigan Territory, to a tiny dot on the map at the outer edge of the known world. The small island is seemingly adrift between two enormous freshwater seas known as Lake Michigan and Lake Huron. The island, along with its village and fort, are called Michilimackinac. To the native inhabitants, the word means "Island of the Great Turtle Spirit," which tells me of its ancient culture—and warns me of the primitive conditions into which I will soon be cast.

The year is 1812, but the following tale commences not with me—nor even with my parents. It begins, rather, in a nearby place—and a far different time. Its main character is a very important person—a young man of whom I am very proud. His name is Peter Jenkins. He is my great-great-great-grandson.

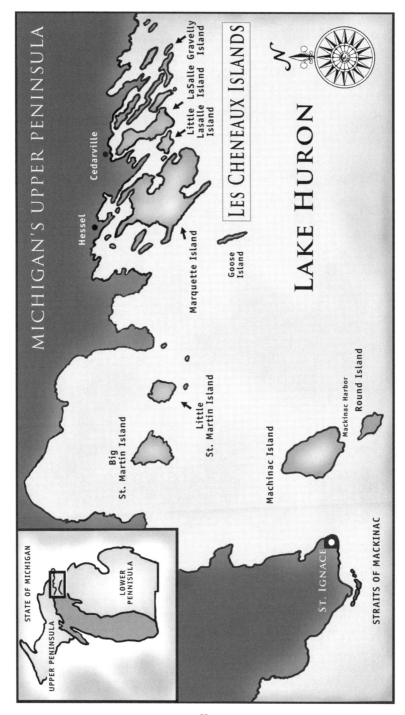

MICHIGAN'S UPPER PENINSULA

LES CHENEAUX ISLANDS

LAKE HURON

Gravelly Island
LaSalle Island
Little LaSalle Island
Lasalle Island
Little Lasalle Island

Cedarville

Hessel

Marquette Island

Goose Island

Big St. Martin Island

Little St. Martin Island

Machinac Island

Mackinac Harbor
Round Island

STATE OF MICHIGAN

UPPER PENINSULA

LOWER PENINSULA

ST. IGNACE

STRAITS OF MACKINAC

v

The Fort At Mackinac Island

CHAPTER 1
TOUR OF THE FORT
AUGUST 27, 1952

"Hello! Earth to Pete!" Kate Hinken chirped playfully. "Are you in there?"

"Yeah, come on, Pete," Dan Hinken urged. "It's our last day here. What do you want to do?"

The morning sun shone brightly on their West Bluff cottage porch. Pete Jenkins lounged in his oversized, brown wicker chair, holding a glass of milk in one hand and a half-eaten jelly doughnut in the other. He turned to Kate, whose blue eyes were sparkling as she awaited his answer. She downed her orange juice in one gulp and glanced at Dan, her twin brother.

Dan was polishing off a cinnamon Danish when he caught Kate's eye. The twins were not in the habit of sitting around when they might be out on North America's most amazing island. The two were regular visitors at their aunt and uncle's summer home. Name it, and they were ready. But now they were waiting for their guest to make up his mind. They had decided that this morning would be Pete's turn to call the shots.

Over the past two weeks, Kate had taken them to all

1

the Island's geological sites. The three had climbed over, under, around and through Chimney Rock, Sugar Loaf and Skull Cave, to name just a few. On the other days, Dan had led them to his favorite historic spots: British Landing, Hubbard's Annex, Fort Holmes and Robinson's Folly. Between the two, Pete had covered nearly every square inch of the Island and had done everything both on and off the chamber of commerce's list of recommended activities—mostly off.

It wasn't as if Pete was new to Michigan's upper peninsula. He'd been crossing the straits and staying at his family's small cabin every summer since he was five, but he had never come to Mackinac Island. "Too expensive," his dad had always said. And it was. "The ferry ride alone costs more than the Island is worth," his dad would say. Which was not true, but it was close enough for his dad, so Pete never went. But that didn't keep him from dreaming about it.

That was before. This summer was different. Pete's chance meeting with the twins early in June had changed everything. They had invited him into their social circle and included him in all their picnics, games and parties. Two weeks ago Dan had asked Pete if he could come with them for a few days at their relatives' place on Mackinac. "You're kidding!" Pete had answered eagerly. He then asked cautiously, "How much will it cost?"

"It's for free, of course," Kate had answered. "We'll sail over in the *Griffin*—Dan and Kate's 25-foot sailboat—and stay with Aunt and Uncle." Pete didn't have to be asked twice.

— — — — —

Doughnut in hand, Pete sat in his chair, desperately trying to think of something that would interest Kate while having it be safe enough that he might actually live to tell the tale. "Uh, well, I don't know," he said. "What *haven't* we done?"

"We haven't ridden our horses blindfolded across Arch Rock," Kate suggested.

Pete wasn't sure if she was kidding. He had never thought of himself as being chicken when it came to a dare, but neither of these two—Kate especially—had any regard for life or limb. Pete realized he'd better think of something fast before her Arch Rock idea caught on.

"You know," Pete said slowly, "when we first sailed into the harbor, that old fort on the bluff caught my eye. How 'bout we poke around in there for awhile?"

"Fort Mackinac?" Kate said, looking dismayed. "There's not much to do." She paused for a moment and then explained, "It's just a bunch of old houses and buildings and stuff."

"It *does* have a lot of history," Dan said, sounding somewhat supportive. "But it's not even really open or anything."

At that, Kate jumped to her feet and turned to her brother. "No, Dan!" she said excitedly. "That's a great idea! Remember the neat way we found to get in?"

Dan stared blankly at his sister. Then a light went on. "You mean the tree?" he asked. She nodded eagerly. "Oh, okay. Sure," Dan said.

"All right! Let's do it," Kate prodded. "I mean, what can happen?"

Pete was immediately stricken by Kate's sudden interest. Ordinarily, when someone said, "What can happen?" it meant, "Hey, no problem." But when Kate

3

said it, it was more of a challenge—like, "How can we turn this otherwise ordinary event into a death-defying stunt?" Pete's mind was reeling. "What have I done?" All he wanted to do was rummage around in an old fort, but Kate's eagerness made it clear that his idea would be a major source of bodily peril.

He had seen that same fire in her eyes a few days ago when she had suggested they go horseback riding on some of Mackinac's trails. Pete had never so much as *sat* on a horse, much less ridden one. He was surprised to hear himself say, "Yeah, that'd be fun." Actually, it had gone pretty well, until the route Kate had led them on took a turn onto a narrow ledge—along a cliff that dropped two hundred feet into Lake Huron's boulder-strewn shore. How he had survived *that*, he would never know.

Kate's devil-may-care enthusiasm once again popped up when she decided they should borrow her uncle's dinghy and go to Round Island. Again, fine—except that the course their small boat took went directly through the busiest shipping lane in the entire world. Seven-hundred-foot-long freighters churned the waters creating enormous wakes. Passenger ferries regularly chugged to and from the mainland. Pleasure boats of all sorts darted across their path.

Pete had only barely endured that little outing when Kate next proposed a game of golf. That sounded safe enough. But on Wawashkamo's fifth hole, Pete hooked his drive out of bounds. The three trekked into the woods and found the ball right at the door of an old barn, which, of course, Kate had to explore. That, in turn, entailed climbing a rickety ladder to a loft where they found a box filled with mysterious papers—and lots of money. She couldn't be happy to leave that unresolved—not without a merry chase from Mackinac to Round Island to capture a bunch of thieves.

So, Pete reasoned, if something bad could come from snooping around an old fort, Kate was sure to make it happen. He wished he had thought of something else for the morning's activity—like sleeping in.

Kate stood in front of Pete's chair, her long, blond hair flowing in the fresh breeze. She motioned to Dan. "Come on. We can be there and back by lunch. Aunt and Uncle won't even miss us."

"All right," Dan said as he hopped from his chair, "but we have to set sail for the Snows by one. Dad told us not to be late for the beach party."

"Oh, you know we can make it," Kate said eagerly. "Three hours with any wind at all will get us there. We'll have plenty of time for the fort."

In the next moment, Dan and Kate, followed by Pete, were hurrying through the spacious summer home. They charged out the back door and into the horse barn. Dan grabbed a coil of rope, and they all hopped on their Schwinns. Kate led the way along the dusty trail behind Grand Hotel toward the high bluff overlooking the harbor. In five minutes the three were leaning their bikes against some lilac bushes.

From where they stood, Pete gazed over the wall onto the grounds of Fort Mackinac and saw several old buildings in various stages of neglect. Tall weeds choked the central courtyard where soldiers had once drilled.

Dan nudged Pete as they stared at the closed gate. "Mr. Porter—he's a friend of my uncle—he brought us here once. We were maybe ten or eleven. He told us that right where we're standing the British fired a cannon back in 1812. The shot went off, beginning what he called 'the Forgotten War.'

"The guy in charge for the Americans was Lieutenant

Hanks. He stood right over there," Dan said, pointing into the fort parade grounds. "That blast was his first clue that England and the United States were at war. Hanks looked up here and saw hundreds of Indians and British soldiers all set to storm the fort and wipe him out. The British guy, Captain Roberts, yelled, 'Give up, or you're toast!'—something like that. Then a bunch of people whose names even Mr. Porter didn't know—a truce party, anyway—came down this hill. Hanks saw the size of the enemy force. It was a no-brainer. He tossed in the towel without firing a shot. Now, that isn't so surprising. He knew his soldiers wouldn't have a chance. But then an amazing thing happened. Somehow—and this is the amazing part—even with this huge number of enemy soldiers and Indians itching to take whatever they could from the fort and the village, not one person was hurt. Not one building was damaged on the whole island. Mr. Porter says that there isn't one other time in history that an army has taken a fort and no one was killed or anything destroyed."

Kate stepped between Dan and Pete. "Come on," she said, grabbing Pete's arm. "Enough chitchat. Let's go."

Pete quickly scanned the fort's high walls. "So, how do we get in?" he asked, looking puzzled. He suddenly remembered that Dan had mentioned a tree.

"Well," Dan replied with a knowing smile, "we *could* go all the way down the hill into town, hire a tour guide with a key and then climb about a thousand steps to the front entrance, which would take the rest of the morning . . ."

"*Or* we could just hop the wall," Kate said with a wink.

"Hop the wall?" Pete said, scanning the entire barricade. "Where? It's got to be twenty feet high!"

"At the last place you'd think," Kate said slyly. She set off across the field, running toward the tallest part of the fort. Dan, with his coil of rope, was right behind her. Pete hurried to keep up. "Right here," she said as she stopped next to an immense pine. The base stood six feet from the wall.

"You're kidding, right?" Pete said.

Kate glanced in all directions; then she scurried up the tree like a scared squirrel. She was nearly at the top when she leaned over. The top of the tree swayed toward the fort. She grabbed the ledge and pulled herself closer. With an acrobatic flip, she disappeared over the wall. A moment later, standing on the rampart, she announced to the boys below, "Okay! The coast is clear!"

Pete's jaw hung open. *The coast is clear for what? She can't honestly think I'm going to do that!*

"Go ahead," Dan said. "I'll watch for the park ranger."

"Park ranger!" Pete exclaimed. "This isn't illegal, is it?"

"I don't know about *illegal*," Dan answered with a shrug. "I mean, they have tours of the place for money. This back gate is kept locked to keep people from having parties here at night and making a mess."

Pete shook his head and looked up at the towering wall. Kate was smiling encouragingly, so he sighed and began to shinny up the tree. He had never been much for high places, being more of a two-feet-on-the-ground sort of guy, but with Kate around, he found he could do some pretty incredible things. So, Pete thought, *why not add "Climb a tree and free-fall into a fort" to the ever-growing list of things I would never do if it weren't for her?*

He was dizzy by the time he got halfway up the tree, and when he looked down from the top, he nearly puked. He leaned toward the fort as Kate had done, and the tree began to sway back and forth. On the last swing, he lunged for the wall. He grabbed the edge and rolled backwards onto the rampart, turning over and landing on his back with a thud. He stood up, faced Kate and said casually, "Piece of cake." He tried to sound nonchalant, but his eyes betrayed him.

Dan next went up, tied the rope to the top of the tree, and then followed the others over the wall. He secured the other end of the rope to the rampart, and soon the three were walking along the wall, twenty feet above the fort grounds. They soon came to a plank stairway and, carefully avoiding the rotten boards, descended to the fort grounds. "Here we are," Kate said cheerfully.

Pete glanced in all directions. The wood buildings were unpainted, their roofs bowed or totally collapsed. The stone ones were losing their mortar, and cobbles were lying all about. Every window and door had been smashed and broken down. Brambles and thorny briars choked the grounds.

"It sure doesn't look like this from the harbor," Pete said. "Doesn't anyone take care of it?"

"The front wall gets whitewashed now and then, but that's just for show," Dan answered. "Mr. Porter says there's a plan to fix the whole place up, but who knows when that'll happen? Come on, I'll show you around. This is the officers' quarters," he said, moving to the nearest stone structure. Without hesitating, he stepped over a battered door and into the room. "Mr. Porter says that this is where Lieutenant Hanks stayed before the British attack."

"What happened to him?" Pete asked.

"You mean Lieutenant Hanks?"

"Yeah," Pete said.

"Don't know," Dan answered. "Probably got sent to prison camp."

Pete tiptoed over a broken windowpane. Shards of glass crunched under his sneakers. He slipped around a smashed billiard table and over a fallen cabinet. As he moved past a hole in the floor, something between the rotted planks caught his eye. He reached down and picked up a weathered, leather-bound book about the size of a pocket dictionary. He opened it and saw faint scribbling on its pages. He was about to toss it back into the hole when he noticed some gold etching on the book's spine. That made it look important, so, with Dan and Kate moving ahead to the next room, he shoved it into his hip pocket and hurried to catch up. He could read it later.

In every room he saw silent reminders—a torn hat, a stocking, a worn-out boot—things that belonged to soldiers who had served at this remote outpost a century before.

"What started it?" Pete asked.

"The war?" Dan responded.

"Yeah," Pete answered. "You don't hear much about it in school. It's like, after the Revolutionary War, people just started moving west, and pretty soon there were 48 states and the country was filled up with people. We must have trounced 'em pretty good."

"Not really," Dan said. "But what's really weird, according to Mr. Porter, is that Fort Mackinac was where the war both began and ended."

Pete shrugged. "It's still ancient history," he said. "I mean, 1812? Who cares?"

9

"Well, some people get into it," Dan said. "Come on, I'll show you the other places—the barracks, the blockhouses, the mess hall. Then we should probably get back for lunch."

After the tour, they went up the stairs to the rampart. With Dan's rope to help, getting out of the fort and back down the tree was a lot easier than getting in. They retrieved their bikes, had lunch with the Andersons and then packed for their sail. Soon, they were aboard the *Griffin* and off on the seventeen-mile voyage to their own cottages on Big LaSalle Island.

CHAPTER 2
RETURN TO THE SNOWS

Pete leaned against a boat cushion and felt the sun on his face. The *Griffin* was on a starboard tack passing Marquette Island when he felt an uncomfortable lump in his hip pocket. He reached back and pulled out the tattered book he'd found that morning.

Kate, sitting next to him, peered over his shoulder. "What's that?" she asked.

"Some kind of a book, I guess," Pete answered. "Maybe a diary or something. I didn't get a chance to open it yet. I picked it up at the fort." He began leafing through the pages but stopped suddenly, staring at an entry. He nudged Kate. "Hey, check this," he said, pointing to the top of a page. "Look! It's dated July 8, 1812!"

Kate leaned closer. "It's an accounts book," she said. "See? 'Sailor's boots, clothes & bedding, £1 2s 1/2d.' And there's someone's name. Looks like Sergeant Skoggs or Skaggs or something. Hey, that was during the War of 1812!"

"Let me see," Dan said eagerly from his place at the *Griffin*'s helm. Pete handed it to him. "This must have belonged to the fort quartermaster," Dan said.

"What's a quartermaster?" Pete asked.

"He's the guy who takes care of all the fort's stuff," Dan said. "He doles out uniforms, guns—all that."

" 'Sailor's boots'?" Pete questioned. "Why would a soldier be needing sailor's boots?"

"Good point," Dan said. He stared at the entry again. "Maybe it came from a ship."

11

"And what's with the funny-looking '£'? What's an 'S' and 'D'?" Pete asked.

"I bet it's from a British ship," Kate answered. "In England they use pounds, shillings and pence, £, S and D, instead of dollars and cents. The whole system is impossible."

Dan handed the book back to Pete, who flipped a few sheets ahead until he was staring at the bottom of a page. It read,

14 July, 1812.

D. Hinken, sailor's slops, 4s 2d   shoes and hose 1d   bedding loaned   Rtd

K. Hinken, sailor's slops, 4s 2d   shoes and hose 1d   bedding loaned   Rtd

"Is this weird or what?" Pete said. He passed the book to Kate and pointed to the entry. "Did you have family here back then?"

Kate stared at the page. "No . . . not that I know of," she answered hesitantly. She handed it to her brother. "What do you make of this, Dan?"

Dan stared silently. "I don't know," he said, finally. "Hinken's a pretty common name. We *could* be related."

Dan returned the book to Pete. Then, checking the course and wind direction, he called, "Ready about!"

Pete stuffed the book into his hip pocket and joined Kate as she scrambled to the other side of the *Griffin*.

"Hard alee!" Dan said. Kate popped a halyard from its cleat, letting the mainsail whip freely in the breeze. Dan pushed the tiller, and all three ducked as the boom whistled over their heads.

"Bitt the halyard!" Dan called. Kate quickly jammed another rope into a different cleat. She pulled the line, hand over hand, until wind filled the mainsail. The sloop heeled, its starboard gunwale nearly touching the rushing water. Pete and Kate leaned way out over the port side to balance the boat.

The new heading placed the *Griffin* on a course that would pass the eastern tip of Marquette Island and shoot her directly down the center of Middle Entrance. The brisk northwesterly wind had made quick work of the seventeen-mile sail.

From here, the three sailors would be busy tacking up the channel to Big LaSalle Island. Even though the sail had been smooth across Lake Huron, Pete was glad to be within the safe confines of the Snows' narrow channels where the average depth was fifteen feet—and not four hundred as it was on the open water. Soon, the *Griffin* approached its home—the red double boathouse on Cincinnati Row. Pete looked eagerly toward the crowd that had gathered. The reception party had already begun. Adults and children in their best beach outfits mingled along the shore.

The Les Cheneaux Islands, or the Snows, as it was known by the resorters, had been the vacation hideaway for well-to-do Cincinnati families since the 1800s. No expense was spared to ensure that each summer was better than the one before. They brought entire staffs of servants—chefs, maids and nannies—to cater to their every whim. Each family owned spacious summer homes and cruised the islands in handsome yachts.

The cottagers at Pete's end of the island were not so well off. Ten years ago Pete's parents had inherited a tiny cabin in a bay well beyond the Cincinnati Row summer homes. Their place had no running water—except when it rained—and no electricity. There were no maids to make the beds—no cooks to prepare their meals. Every day Pete and his sister, Cara, would hop aboard their tiny aluminum boat with its three-and-a-half-horsepower motor and snail their way past the Cincinnati Row boathouses into town for mail and groceries.

It was a bit humbling but, in spite of that, Pete couldn't have been happier. He knew that back home in Saginaw his friends were baking on flat playgrounds while he merrily hiked, swam and fished in this resort paradise. Still, he couldn't help but watch in awe and some envy as the Cincinnati kids skied and sailed around the bays and channels.

But that was all in the past. *This* summer, due to a wonderful stroke of luck, Pete had met Dan and Kate. They quickly introduced him to their friends, and before long Pete's days were filled with parties, picnics, long sails—things he'd never done in his life. It was the best summer he had ever had.

-    -   -   -   -

With Kate and Pete ready to make the lines fast, Dan guided the *Griffin* close to the red double boathouse. On shore, the entourage of smartly dressed resorters moved from the beach to the wide dock to greet the returning sailors. Among the crowd, Pete saw his mom, dad and sister. In their denim jeans and plain shirts, they stood out like bluebells in a field of chrysanthemums. Kate dropped the mainsail and gathered it in. Pete scooted out over the bow and snapped a line to the mooring ball. With that, the extended voyage of the *Griffin* was officially over.

Dr. and Mrs. Hinken had prepared a grand homecoming for their twins. They invited, of course, the entire Cincinnati Row crowd but also Pete's family from the other end of the island. The Hinkens' hired staff scurried about, completing the final touches that transferred the sandy shore into a magnificent party setting.

Pete spotted a table at the edge of the beach. It was groaning with salad bowls and dessert trays. Nearby, steaks, ribs and hamburgers sizzled over a glowing fire pit.

When their dinghy touched the dock, Pete hopped out of the boat and hugged his mother. "How was Mackinac Island?" she bubbled. "You've got to tell me all about it."

"It was great," Pete answered. "The whole place is amazing!"

Pete's dad stepped forward. "I hope you won't mind your dull old cottage for another few days," he said. "From what we've heard, it doesn't compare with the Andersons' place on Mackinac."

"No," Pete said, "but believe me, it's great to be home." He glanced at the feast along the shore. People were lining up at the food tables. "I'm starved," he said. "Let's dig in."

Kate

CHAPTER 3
AN INVITATION

Shadows were lengthening as Pete and his sister stood alone by the campfire. He was telling her about how he, Dan and Kate had catapulted themselves over the twenty-foot-high wall into Fort Mackinac.

Most of the guests had left, heading to their cottages along Cincinnati Row. Pete's parents were at the edge of the clearing, thanking Dr. and Mrs. Hinken for inviting them to the party. Kate came to Pete's side. Dan was with her. "Tomorrow is Mr. Heuck's Pirate Party," Dan said. "Want to come?"

"What kind of party?" Pete asked.

"Pirate Party," Dan repeated. "Every year we all dress up like pirates and meet at Mr. Heuck's boathouse for breakfast. Then around noon we board his old scow, the *Captain Bing,* and he takes us to some uninhabited island for a picnic and treasure hunt. He hides stuff all over the place and then leaves clues for us to find them."

"Oh, Pete!" Kate exclaimed. Her smile was dazzling. "Do say you will. It's great fun."

Pete tore his eyes from Kate and stared at Dan. "This isn't something where the pirates occasionally get clobbered or anything, is it?" he asked. He'd learned that, with Dan and Kate, nothing was ever as harmless as it sounded. His morning's visit to Fort Mackinac was reminder enough of that.

"Don't be silly," Kate said with a laugh. "It's an old tradition, something Mr. Heuck started ages ago. It's sort of an end-of-summer party for kids. Nobody over

17

twenty can come." Kate glanced at Cara. "You're both invited. Oh, please say yes."

"I think you'd better count me out," Cara replied. "On my last trip to Never-Never Land, I promised Tinker Bell I'd stay out of pirate affairs. But my little brother here, Peter Pain, he might want to come."

Pete scowled at his sister and turned to Kate. His mind had been made up the moment she had asked, but he didn't want to seem too eager. "Well, I guess," he said, "So, there aren't any real pirates?" he added with a laugh.

"Not unless you count Mr. Heuck," Dan said. "He puts on his Captain Hook outfit and acts as scary as he can. Everyone gets into costume. Do you have any old-fashioned clothes?"

Cara answered for her little brother. "Leave that to me," she said. "Pete will be the best buccaneer aboard."

Pete glanced at Cara, anxiety written all over his face. "That's right," he said, turning to Kate. "Leave it to my big sister to humiliate me before I even get started."

"So, you'll come?" Kate asked.

Pete nodded. "I'll have to ask my parents, but I'm sure they'll say it's okay."

"You're in for a treat," Dan said. "Be down at our place at a quarter to nine. We'll walk to Mr. Heuck's boathouse together."

"See you tomorrow, Pete," Kate said with a wave. "We've got to run. Dan and I have to go into town and get the mail."

At that, Pete and his sister turned and hurried to catch up with their parents, who were walking along the shoreline trail back to their cabin.

"And just what do you have in mind for pirate

18

clothes?" Pete asked, eyeing Cara suspiciously.

"You'll see," Cara said with a sly grin.

\-   -   -   -   -

You'll see was an expression Pete had learned long ago to regard as a bad omen—one that often preceded a fate worse than death. On Pete's first day of kindergarten, Cara had switched his jeans with a pair of her old ones—pants that buttoned up the side. Pete was in such a rush to get going that he didn't notice the switch until he was standing at the front door of Handley School. When the first bell sounded, everyone from kindergarten to sixth grade stopped playing marbles, jacks or skipping rope and rushed to the door. As they crammed the front entrance, a big first-grader gave Pete a push. "Hey! You a boy or a girl?" the kid said.

"I'm a boy!" Pete answered indignantly.

"Then how come you got girl's pants on?" the boy taunted. Pete looked down and saw the hip-side buttons. He heard kids snickering all around. Pete's face burned in embarassment. He had to do something fast. As the boy was snorting haughtily to the others, Pete wound up and popped him square on the nose. Blood flowed. A dozen pairs of long legs came out of nowhere, and the two boys were snatched up and whisked inside. Pete was on the carpet, facing the principal about two minutes before his academic career officially began.

\-   -   -   -   -

It was late afternoon when Pete led his parents and sister along the winding, tree-lined Cincinnati Row trail. He hurried past the grand boathouses on his right and the even grander summer homes on his left. Soon they reached the Elliot Hotel, the dividing line between the two socially distinct ends of LaSalle Island.

From there, Pete broke into a dead run along the sun-baked, dusty path until he came to his cottage. There it was, just as it looked two weeks before—a one-story cabin with a bunch of old wicker rocking chairs scattered on its narrow porch. It was the same, all right, but now, somehow, it looked a lot smaller than when he had left.

He ran up the steps, pulled open the screen door and stepped inside. The door closed behind him with a resounding slap. Everything was in place—wood stove, kitchen table, straight-back chairs, oil lanterns. Even the smell was the same—the wonderful odor of kerosene lamps and musty comic books.

He was home and, for Pete, there was no place like it.

CHAPTER 4
PIRATE PETE'S NEW CLOTHES

Pete visited the outhouse, and when he returned he passed his father in the kitchen, filling the kindling box next to the stove. He went on into the living room where his mom was trimming the wick on a reading lamp. She settled into her cushy rocker and opened a book.

"So, you had a nice time on Mackinac Island?" she asked.

"It was great," Pete answered. "I did more stuff in two weeks—the place is amazing."

Mr. Jenkins joined them. He sat in his easy chair and put his feet up on the hassock. "So, I expect you'll be wanting to spend a little quiet time around here," he said. "We'll be heading home in three days. School starts the day after that."

"Well, yeah, sort of," Pete answered. "But tomorrow, Dan and Kate have invited me to a picnic. It's just for kids. Everybody gets dressed up like pirates, and Mr. Heuck takes them out on some old boat of his to an island somewhere. They've been doing it for years. Okay if I go?"

"Seems fine to me," Mr. Jenkins said. "This isn't going to get dangerous like some of your other outings, is it?"

Just then Pete's sister came in. Pete looked her way. "They invited Cara, too," Pete said, "but she didn't want to come. It didn't sound dangerous to you, did it?"

"No more than sailing or water skiing," Cara said with

21

a wink, knowing how Pete had barely survived his first encounters with each of those two activities.

"All right," Mr. Jenkins said. "You'll be home before dark?"

"Oh, I'm sure," Pete said. "It's just a picnic. So, I can go?"

"As long as you're careful," his mom said with a nod.

"Come on, Pete," Cara said, turning toward the front bedroom. She swept aside the curtain and Pete followed. "Okay," she said, "I know just the outfit. You'll be the best pirate there."

"What *outfit* are you talking about?" Pete asked.

Cara moved to a large cedar chest in the corner. Pete knew it was filled with old clothes, mostly women's, so it wasn't anything he had ever cared to explore. Cara lifted the lid and dug in like a dog for a buried bone. First, she set aside the top layer, mostly 1930s-era women's dresses with high, starchy collars. The next archaeological level was her grandmother's black gowns. Then came carefully preserved relics from around 1900. Pete watched, growing worried that his sister was planning to dress him up like a girl. It wouldn't be the first time.

About halfway through the chest, Cara pulled out a man's blue coat with tarnished brass buttons. She then unfolded a pair of dark blue trousers with black stripes. Pete had seen these in a photo of Great-Grandfather Drake taken on his return from the Civil War. The image of the man's sunken eyes and the outfit's ragged edges had clearly shown that both soldier and uniform had seen better days. But what could this have to do with the pirate party?

Cara wasn't done. She rummaged through more

things—again, mostly women's—long dresses that Pete had seen in tintypes of Great-Grandmother Drake. Finally, she got to the very bottom and held up a black, narrow-brimmed hat, a blue coat, a red-and-white-striped cotton shirt, grey neckerchief, white britches, long white socks, and a pair of black shoes. She turned to Pete and smiled triumphantly.

"What is *that*?" he asked.

"It's your pirate suit," Cara said proudly. "It belonged to Grandpa Drake's great-grandfather."

"He was a pirate?" Pete asked.

"I don't know *that* for sure," Cara answered. "I *do* know he was a sailor when he was young. You don't remember Grampa Drake. He died soon after you were born, but he used to tell us lots of family stories. One was about his great-grampa being taken aboard a British ship during the War of 1812. He was made cabin boy and taken to Mackinac Island."

"How come I never heard any of this?" Pete asked. He took the striped shirt and held it in front of him for size. The mothball smell about knocked him over.

"After Grampa Drake died, I guess it just never came up again," Cara said with a shrug. "He was a real storyteller. Set him down in front of a campfire and he could go on for hours—all the while toasting the best marshmallows ever."

Pete pulled off his white T-shirt and slipped the striped jersey over his head. He checked the mirror and then traded his jeans for the white pants. Finally, he donned the socks, shoes and blue jacket. "I guess everything fits," he said. "Pant legs sure are funny looking."

"They're bell-bottoms," Kate said. "Grampa said that if a sailor went overboard, he could pull them off easier than regular pants—keep him from drowning."

Pete added the hat and neckerchief and stepped again before the mirror. Aside from smelling like a giant mothball, he looked pretty sharp. He noticed something hard in one of the vest pockets. He reached in and pulled out a thick, black coin. It was bigger than a silver dollar. "What's this?" he asked, showing it to his sister.

"I've never seen it before," Cara said, looking amazed. She tossed it a few inches into the air and caught it. "It's heavy enough to be gold!"

"Let's show it to Dad," Pete said.

The two went into the living room where their parents were reading. It was already dark outside. Mr. Jenkins looked up and stared at Pete's uniform. "Where did you get that?" he asked.

"It was at the bottom of the cedar chest," Cara answered. She turned to her mother. "Mom, tell Pete the story—you know, the one about our ancestor—the one whose boat got sunk near Mackinac Island."

"Oh, yes, Will Drake," Averill Jenkins said, looking up from her book. "Hmm. I'll have to think. Will would have been—let me see—my great-great-grandfather. He was born out east, New York City, I believe, around 18 . . .—no, it would have been 1796 or '97. I know that because he was fifteen, and it happened at the very beginning of the War of 1812. He and his parents were sailing to Mackinac Island to live. They were almost there when a British man-o'-war sank their ship. Will was the only survivor. He was taken aboard and made to serve the captain as cabin boy. He was given the uniform you're wearing now. The ship landed at Mackinac Island and Will stayed there. Some time later, he married a Mackinac girl—her name was Averill, same as mine—and they each led very exciting lives. Will became a fur trader and was a friend to many Indian chiefs. He even served with Oliver Hazard Perry against the British on Lake Erie in 1813 to help win the war. They built their home on the island, and she raised their four boys and four girls—all the while entertaining the most important social visitors from all over the world. That's when Mackinac Island was the most important place in the entire Northwest Territory."

Pete handed the tarnished coin to his father. "We found this, too," Pete said. "It was in the jacket pocket."

Mr. Jenkins reached for a magnifying glass that he kept near his chair. He turned the coin over and shined it on his pants. He brought it closer to the light and looked again. "It's a British penny, dated 1811," he said.

"A penny?" Pete said. "It's so big! If a guy carried a quarter's worth of these in his pocket and fell overboard, he'd sink like a rock."

"A penny went a lot farther back then," his dad replied. "He probably wouldn't have had more than one at a time. You know how people stash an extra dollar in their wallet for emergencies? Will Drake may have kept this penny for just such an occasion."

"Look at the clock, Pete," his mother said. "If you're going to be down at your friends' house by nine, you'd better get to bed now. Sounds like you've got a pretty busy day ahead of you."

"Yeah, you're right," Pete said. "Good night." He stuck the penny back in his vest and went to his bedroom. He undressed quickly, hanging his clothes near the open window to air out, and slipped into his pajamas. He dived between his bunk's thick cotton sheets and was asleep in minutes.

During the night, he had a fantastic dream about sailing to Mackinac Island. He was aboard an immense, old-fashioned ship. The year was 1812 and he shared a bunk with a boy exactly his age. But it wasn't just any boy. It was Will Drake. On the same boat were Indians and soldiers, and they sailed through storms and did all sorts of wild things. When he awoke, unlike with other dreams he usually had, which flew out of his head before he could blink, he remembered everything. It was so real—raising sails, scrubbing decks—but mainly he remembered what it was like to be friends with his own great-great-great-grandfather. It was weird and scary and wonderful, all at the same time.

CHAPTER 5
PETE EXPLAINS HIS OUTFIT

The next morning, Pete bounced out of his bunk ready to start the day. After Cara gave her little brother time to don his pirate clothes, she rolled over in her bed and pronounced her opinion. "Looking mighty sharp, Pete."

"Thanks," Pete replied flatly, "but the more I think of it, the more it bugs me. Like as not, everyone else will be in blue jeans and T-shirts, maybe with a bandanna or something. I'll get there, dressed like this, and they'll think I'm some sort of nut."

"Well, they can't fault you for not getting into the act," Cara said.

"I just hope this isn't the most embarrassing day of my life," Pete said as he pulled the black sailor shoes on over the long white socks. Next to his bed, he spotted the mysterious accounts book he'd found at Fort Mackinac. He slid it into his jacket pocket and took one last look in the mirror. Staring back at Pete was a gangly kid with straggly brown hair in a goofy sailor suit. He did not see a preppy, good-looking guy like Dan or any of the others who lived along Cincinnati Row. The image did little to bolster his confidence. He shrugged and stepped into the next room.

He heard his parents talking in the kitchen, so he went in to let them know he was leaving. His father was standing at the wood stove, frying eggs and bacon in a black iron skillet. His mom was pouring coffee into two blue porcelain cups.

"You look great, Pete," his mother said. "I'll bet Will

27

Drake wasn't any more handsome."

"Have some bacon and eggs?" his dad asked. "No pirate ever bounded over the bounding main without a hearty breakfast."

"We're having something at Mr. Heuck's boathouse before we go," Pete said. "Well, I don't want to be late. See you this afternoon." He turned for the front door.

"Be careful," his mom said. Pete could be going to the outhouse in the middle of the afternoon and his mom would say, "Be careful." Still, given his past experiences with Kate and Dan, he decided to take her warning a little more seriously.

Pete nodded and pushed open the front door. He hurried down the flagstone steps to the dusty Elliot Row trail. He felt a little foolish in his sailor suit, so he raced past his neighbors' small cabins and across the front lawn of the Elliot Hotel. He reached the hedgerow separating the two ends of LaSalle Island, lifted a branch leading to the hidden maze and darted ahead.

He emerged moments later in Cincinnati Row. Even now, after a whole summer of being included in the company of the Row's residents, he still felt strangely out of place—like a trespasser. He trotted silently along the twisting trail.

He soon approached the Hinkens' cottage, feeling like an eel that had just slipped through a fisherman's net. Dan and Kate were coming down the path toward him. Kate looked remarkable in her blue shorts, checkered blouse and red neckerchief. Dan was decked out in cut-off jeans, a striped shirt and a blue polka dot bandanna.

Dan waved to Pete and continued toward him. But Kate, on seeing Pete, froze in her tracks. Her face paled as if she were going to faint.

Dan, unaware that his sister had stopped, yelled, "Hey, Pete, great getup! You'll win 'Best Pirate' for sure. It looks real. Where'd you find it?"

"It's kind of a long story," Pete answered quickly, but his gaze lingered on Kate. She still looked dazed. "What's the matter, Kate?" Pete asked. "It's this outfit, isn't it? I'll embarrass you in front of your friends. I can go home and change."

Kate forced a smile. Stepping toward Pete, she answered, "No, no, it's not that," she said. "It's just—I remembered something—something totally impossible— a silly dream I had last night. But it's nothing, honest. No, Pete, you look great." She stood now in front of him, her dazzling smile melting him like a lump of butter in a hot pan. "So, where *did* you get it?"

"It's from an ancestor of mine—my great-great-great-grandfather, Will Drake—he wore it," Pete said. "He was taken aboard a British ship in the War of 1812 and was made to work for the captain. This is what they gave him to wear." Pete turned to Dan. Dan was gaping at his sister, and now *he* was looking as freaked as Kate had a moment before. "Dan! What's wrong?" Pete asked.

Dan continued his startled gaze, staring still at Kate. "Did you say you had a dream?" he asked.

"Yes," she said, returning his surprised look. "But it couldn't be anything."

"I had a dream last night, too," Dan said nervously. "It was like some of those others we've had. You know, like last summer when we each dreamed that our boathouse exploded. We both woke up in the middle of the night and ran down to the dock. That rag smoldering near the *Polly Ann*'s gas tank—if we hadn't gotten there when we did, the boathouse *would* have blown up. Or two weeks ago on Mackinac when we both dreamed that Miss Fisher's house at the Annex was being torched. If we hadn't jumped on our bikes and gone there when we did, she would have died in the fire! My dream last night was like those. I got up and started for your room but stopped at your door. I thought about it and decided that my dream was so impossible that it couldn't be like those others—you know, a warning or whatever."

"What *was* your dream?" Kate asked anxiously.

Dan shook his head. "There was this old sailboat—the kind you see in pirate movies," he began slowly. "The three of us—Pete, you and I—were aboard."

Kate stared grimly at her brother. "A tall ship was in *my* dream, too!" she whispered. "We met a boy who was dressed like Pete is now. That's what startled me just a minute ago. It was during the War of 1812. Why would we be dreaming about *that*? It doesn't make any sense."

"That's what worries me," Dan said. "These dreams never *do* make sense—not until we follow them, at least. Then they make all kinds of sense."

"Well, it can't be like the others this time," Kate said, shaking her head. "We're going to a picnic, not a war. Let's head over to Mr. Heuck's boathouse. He said he wanted us to be the first ones there. I don't know why, but since we are his guests, we should do as he asks." She turned and motioned for Dan and Pete to follow her along the trail.

"Wait a minute," Pete said, getting in step behind Dan. "I keep hearing you talk about this Mr. Heuck. He's beginning to sound like the Pied Piper—the guy who tricked all the kids away from their homes and kept them hostage. What's he like?"

"Oh, there's nothing like that to worry about," Dan said. "He's a bit eccentric sometimes—but a really great guy. In a way, he *is* like the Pied Piper. Years ago, he got all his Cincinnati friends to start coming up here."

"How'd he do that?" Pete asked.

"I think he stumbled across this place on a fishing trip while he was staying on Mackinac Island," Dan answered. "To him, the Snows was like a major slice of heaven, so he bought a few parcels of land. The next year he invited some of his neighbors and family, and pretty soon they were all building cottages along here. That's why it's called Cincinnati Row."

Pete followed Dan and Kate as they made their way along the mossy shoreline trail. They sidestepped some muddy areas and moved past Mr. Heuck's large summer home on their right. To their left, a barrier of eight-foot-tall cattails blocked Cedarville Channel from view. Finally, the path led to a boardwalk, and Pete saw Mr. Heuck's immense, two-story boathouse. He followed the others as they climbed a wide stairway along the outside wall.

Just as they got to the top, the door swung open. Out jumped the scariest-looking man Pete had ever seen. He was short and squat and built like an army truck. He wore a yellow sou'wester, a red shirt, blue pants and black, knee-high boots. Around his waist was a wide black belt. Tucked into that was a long, curved dagger. He was missing two front teeth—an upper and a lower. A black patch over his left eye and a scar on his right cheek bore grim evidence of past sea battles. Balancing himself on a crude crutch, he snarled fiercely into the faces of his three visitors. Pete remembered instantly Kate's description of the party's host, but that didn't matter. He was not about to test this guy.

"Avast, yeh scurvy bunch o' landlubbers!" he shouted, staring at Pete with his one good eye. Pete jumped back and caught himself on the railing, barely saving himself from going down the stairs the fast way. Dan and Kate stifled a howl.

"So, yeh figgered yeh'd sneak up on the old pirate and steal his vittles, did yeh now," the man roared, again making one-eyed contact with Pete—and Pete alone. Pete stood, clinging to the railing, his mouth agape.

Dan stepped forward. "Yes, sir, Captain Heuck, an' yeh better fork 'em over," he said with a growl. Pete thought he heard Kate snicker. He was comforted, somewhat, by her bravado.

"Well, yeh'll not be gettin' one morsel 'til yeh pledge in blood to join me aboard the *Captain Bing*. We'll be needin' twenty more hearties like yourselves to ride the waves of the northern main."

"Aye, they'll be scuttlin' across yer decks afore yeh know," Kate said, affecting a snarl. A malicious sneer accompanied the transformation.

"Oh, will they, now?" Mr. Heuck replied. "And when in the blazes might that be?"

"It'll be soon, Cap'n, but all in good time." Dan too sneered. "And they'll be wantin' some o' them vittles yeh was talkin' about. Me friends an' me—we've sailed all the way from the Dark Isle and have a powerful hunger about us."

The grisly pirate punched a stubby finger into Dan's chest. "Aye, and just who might *you* be?" he asked nastily.

"It's Dangerous Dan, I am." Dan growled. "Arghh, an' this 'ere be Cantankerous Kate, the She-devil o' the Lowland Sea."

"Well, yeh sounds like pirates, sure yeh do," the captain barked. He turned to Pete. He lifted his crutch and poked it an inch from Pete's nose. "An' who would you be?"

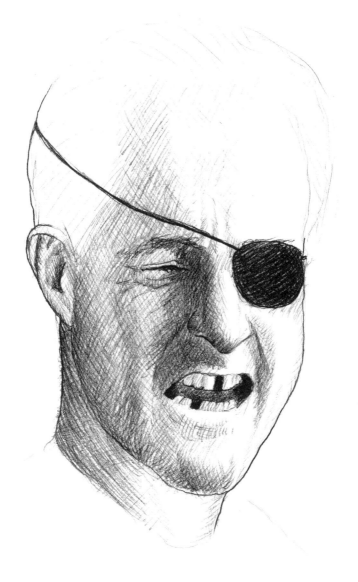

Mr. Heuck

"I'm P-Pete Jenkins, sir," Pete stammered.

"An' are yeh fer me or agin' me, lad?"

"I'm, uh, for you, sir," Pete answered uncertainly.

"See that yeh are, m'boy, or I'll 'ave yeh walkin' the plank soon enuf, sure I will," growled the man.

At that, Mr. Heuck drew himself toward Pete for a closer look at the young sailor. He cocked his good eye within inches of Pete's face. Pete could now see that the pirate's missing teeth were simply blackened gum like actors use onstage. The scar, too, was fake. Still, the man looked plenty capable of executing whatever dastardly acts he might threaten.

Mr. Heuck crutched himself back a step and surveyed Pete, sizing him up. "I see yeh be a limey tar, by the looks of yer garb," he said, correctly assessing the origin of Pete's outfit. "Yeh'd be a seaman, to be sure, and not a horse marine like the sorry lot yeh brung with yeh. How be it yeh come by yer slops, is what I want to know?"

"My 'slops'?" Pete asked.

"Aye, yer gear, boy, yer gear!"

"My clothes?" Pete guessed.

"Arghh," Mr. Heuck grunted with a nod.

"They're from a relative," Pete said. "They belonged to my great-great-great-grandfather."

"Pinched 'em off a dead man, eh?" Mr. Heuck said with a twinkle in his eye. "I like that in a shipmate, arghh, that I do. Welcome aboard and bring yer landlubbin' mates with yeh." At that, he stepped into the Captain's Quarters, as a sign above the door said. He bowed grandly, motioning his guests to enter.

Pete was the first to step over the threshold. What he saw totally amazed him. It was like climbing into a treehouse and finding the Taj Mahal. Pete had passed this boathouse a thousand times in his aluminum outboard, the *Tiny Tin*, each time wondering what was up there. He had imagined it was like his cabin, plain but livable. Instead, it was an entire spectacular house! Kitchen, bathroom, two bedrooms and an enormous, lavishly furnished living room decorated with all sorts of nautical stuff—ancient globes, harpoons, wooden mermaids and ships' spars. Above the kitchen door, a sign read Galley. Over the bathroom was the word Head, and so it went throughout the fantastic boathouse home.

"Arghh," Mr. Heuck said, nodding toward the kitchen. "The grub's in the galley. Yeh'll find the standard fare, sure yeh will. There's burgoo in the kettle and lobscouse in the pot. There's dandyfunk, poor jack and dried horse," he said pointing at different places in the kitchen. "An' the bucket yonder's got yer lime juice. Yeh can't go t' sea without yer flagon o' lime."

At the sound of the bill of fare, Pete suddenly wished he'd taken his dad up on the bacon and eggs. When he followed Kate into the kitchen, however, his eyes lit up. Before him on a wide table was a monstrous platter of sausages. Next to that were mounds of scrambled eggs, piles of French toast and all sorts of fresh fruit. There were pitchers of orange juice and milk. Another table was loaded with Danish pastries, sticky buns and doughnuts. Who was this guy trying to kid? Even more—what army was he planning to feed?

Pete soon found out. He heard a bold knock at the door and glanced into the living room. Neal Preston was leading the Marquette Island crowd past a smiling Mr. Heuck. Each newcomer was dressed in an outfit befitting a mutiny on the Barbary Coast. In minutes, the place was packed with kids, some as young as six—some as old as twenty. The noise was deafening.

All of them were doing their best to talk and act as pirate-y as they could. For the first time, Pete relaxed. He knew that Captain Heuck couldn't make them all walk the plank.

CHAPTER 6
BOARDING THE *CAPTAIN BING*

With his crutch held high above his head, Captain Heuck nimbly leaped from the floor to a chair. He then waved his hands over his head to get the attention of his guests. "Arghh! Avast, mateys!" he bellowed to the raucous crowd. The hooting and hollering stopped immediately. "I see by me ship's timepiece," he said, glancing at his watch, "that we're due to board our vessel and sail the seas for glorious plunder. Arghh, rich merchant craft be plying these waters, sure they be, their holds a-bulging with doubloons and pieces of eight. What say ye, lads and lasses? Are yeh with me?"

"Aye, aye, Captain!" came the resounding reply.

"First, you'll be tidyin' the galley, swabbin' the deck an' makin' this old scow shipshape, like it was when yeh found 'er," Mr. Heuck ordered. "An' you'll be quick about yer duties, yeh will, or me name's not Mad Cap'n Heuck!"

Instantly, the crew jumped into action. The young privateers laughed and jabbered in their best pirate jargon as they did. Some washed the dishes, some dried, some put them away. Kate grabbed a Hoover, and Pete helped by moving the furniture as she swabbed the deck. Before long, the place was clean as a bosun's whistle.

"Ahoy!" Captain Heuck called. "Step lively, mates. Grab a life jacket and hurry down to the ship." He handed baskets of food and jugs of drink to each member of the crew—heavy ones for the bigger buccaneers and lighter ones for the small—but

37

everyone carried something down the stairs from the Captain's Quarters to the dock. There, inside the boathouse, festooned with nautical flags from stem to stern, was the *Captain Bing*. A huge black-and-white Jolly Roger waved from the rear flagstaff.

Pete had seen this old, double-ended, gray boat on the water many times, always carrying a crowd of people, but he had never actually been aboard. As he stepped onto the gunnel, he realized how sturdy it was. Its steel hull was twenty-five feet long and measured eight feet at the beam. The *Captain Bing* had been a U.S. Navy lifeboat and Mr. Heuck had refitted it with an inboard, 28-horsepower engine. The transformation instantly converted the ungainly vessel into Les Cheneaux resorters' favorite party place—one that would provide fond memories of grand occasions for generations to come.

This would be one of those days—certainly for Dan, Kate and Pete.

"Careful, lads," Captain Heuck called as he stepped from the dock onto the boat. "Take care stowin' them vittles. Yeh'd get mighty hungry out there if yeh deep-six 'em now."

Dan was next to board and Pete followed. Each took the hands of the older girls in turn. The other boys stood amidships and hoisted the smaller kids onto the spacious *Bing*. In less than a minute, all twenty were seated or standing in the unusual vessel.

"All aboard!" Mr. Heuck called as he pulled the starting crank on the old, single-stroke engine. Nothing happened. "Curses!" he snarled. He repositioned himself and tried a second time. No response. "Blast!" he roared. "She's cold, she is. Hasn't been out in a couple o' days," he added. He then bent way down and put both hands on the crank. He pulled mightily, and the motor responded with a low-pitched chug . . . chug . . . chug. Pete could feel as well as hear the belches come from deep within the *Bing*'s innards.

Mr. Heuck let the engine run for a minute and then moved to the helm. He hoisted himself up to a wide, cushioned bench and pulled a wooden lever backwards. The *Bing* eased out of the boathouse. He spun the wheel and pushed the knob ahead. Soon the craft was pointed toward Cedarville Harbor.

He then slid another lever to its peak, and the engine responded with only a slightly faster-paced and higher-pitched chug-chug-chug-chug. This, Pete realized, was full throttle. The Pirate Party would move no faster than trolling speed. Pete glanced over the side to check the water, privately wishing he'd brought his rod and reel. He'd never fished this far from his cottage.

Mr. Heuck guided the *Bing* around Ailes Point to the other side of LaSalle Island. From there, he kept Island Number Eight on his port and Government Island to his starboard. Finally, he eased the *Bing* through the Boot Island Pass and out into Lake Huron. From a small compartment next to the wheel, Captain Heuck pulled an old-fashioned brass spyglass. He extended the device and scanned the horizon. The *Bing* chugged into open water where the waves rolled in long swells, even on a calm day such as this.

In the *Bing*'s bow, some of the kids were belting out "Sixteen Men on a Dead Man's Chest," while others jabbered their pirate slang at each other. Meanwhile, Pete sat alone near Mr. Heuck and watched as he worked the levers and directed the *Bing* farther into the lake. Just when Pete was sure the captain was indeed taking them away forever like the Pied Piper, Mr. Heuck turned the wheel and steered the boat in a large circle

39

back toward the islands.

"I've got something to take care of at the bow, Pirate Pete," Captain Heuck said, glancing toward him. He stood and made room at his bench. "You've been watching me handle this 'ere ship. Would yeh be a good mate an' mind the helm for a bit?"

"Sure," Pete said, surprised to be asked. He moved over into the captain's seat.

"Just keep the tip of that 'ere point o' land straight off our bow," Mr. Heuck ordered. "That be Treasure Island, sure it be."

"Yes, sir," Pete said. Only the faintest sign of land showed on the horizon.

As the captain went forward, Kate made her way back and sat beside Pete. "You've been pretty quiet," she said. "Everything okay?"

Pete held the wheel with one hand, looking as captainly as he could. "Oh, yeah. Great. How 'bout you?"

"You just seemed sort of distant," Kate said, taking his left hand in hers.

Pete's suntanned cheeks took on an immediate cast of pink. "Yeah, well, you know," he stammered. "I've just been thinking, that's all."

"About what?" she said with a squeeze.

With Kate snuggling up to his side and holding his hand, Pete's brain went completely blank. He could think of nothing but her. He sputtered for a moment, "Oh, you know, just thinking—great day, neat party, stuff like that."

"I've been thinking, too," Kate said. "I've been wondering about my dream last night . . . being aboard that old sailing ship . . . how much you look like the boy who was in it. At first, I thought it *was* you—

except he had longer hair."

Pete blinked. Kate had been dreaming about him!

"And yet he couldn't have been you, could he?" she continued, "being in 1812, I mean."

"I guess not," Pete said, his voice falling.

"I've been wondering," she said softly. "Maybe it had something to do with that book you found at the fort— the accounts book. That was so weird about the entry for D. and K. Hinken. Maybe that's the reason Dan and I had such similar dreams last night."

"But that wouldn't explain why I was in it, too," Pete said.

"I think it does," Kate offered. "I think it's because you found the book."

Pete shrugged. "Could be," he said. "Oh, I started to tell you back at your place. I had a sailing dream last night, too. I only remembered it when you told me about yours. My dreams never make much sense—as least not the next morning when I try to figure them out. But the one last night was different. I dreamed I was sailing in an old ship with my great-great-great-grandfather—like we were buddies." Pete reached into his vest pocket. "Anyway, I brought this with me."

"The accounts book?" Kate asked, looking intently as he drew it from his jacket. "Why'd you bring that?"

Pete shrugged. "I don't know. It was next to my bed when I was putting on these clothes. It just seemed to go with it. I thought it could be something we'd show the other kids." He handed it to Kate.

She thumbed through the pages and found the July 14th entry where her namesake was listed. She flipped back a page and studied that one as well. Suddenly, she jumped to her feet. "What did you say his name was?"

"Who?" Pete asked, startled by Kate's sudden burst

of interest.

"Your ancestor!" she said, looking alarmed. "The one whose uniform you're wearing!"

"Oh, uh . . . Will Drake," Pete answered. "Why?"

Kate pushed the book in front of Pete. "Look at this," she said.

Pete took his eye off the point on Gravelly Island. He looked carefully at the page where Kate was pointing. It read:

14 July, 1812

Lake Huron—between Bois Blanc and St. Mary's River

W. Drake   Sailor's slops,   4s 6d   shoes & hose 1d   bedding loaned

Pete stared for several moments. He nodded as if completing a mental puzzle. "That's got to be him!" he whispered. Now it was Pete's turn to look spooked. Finally, he added, "It fits with what my mom told me. The British sank the boat that Will and his parents were taking to Mackinac Island. Everyone aboard died, except for him. That must be why his name is the only entry in the accounts book for that date!"

"What this means," Kate said as she handed the book back to Pete, "is that your ancestor, and maybe some of mine, were aboard the same ship in 1812!"

"That is *too* weird!" Pete said. He took his eyes from the book and looked into the distance. His reverie was interrupted when he noticed that the *Bing* was closing in on Gravelly Island. He shoved the book into his vest pocket and checked down the throttle.

Mr. Heuck was making his way past the other kids to the helm. "Well done, Pirate Pete," he said, resuming his place at the wheel. "I'll take 'er in from here, but stand by. I may need your help soon." He looked forward and called to the bow. "Ahoy! Dangerous Dan! Report to the helm!" To the others he ordered, "Roll up your pants and take off yer socks and shoes. The biggest of yeh can get off first and help the smaller buccaneers ashore."

At that, he set the engine gear to neutral, and the *Bing* coasted to the beach. A gentle crunch of pebbles against the steel hull signaled their arrival. "All right, step lively now," Mr. Heuck called. "All ashore that's going ashore."

The older boys jumped from the bow into the shallow water, holding the *Bing* in place. "Be a good mate and pass over the cargo," Duke called in his best Long John Silver lingo. The older girls laughed and formed a bucket brigade, handing the baskets to the shore crew.

Kate and Dan stayed with Pete and Captain Heuck in the stern as their fellow pirates disembarked.

"Just as I feared," Mr. Heuck said, appraising the situation. "I don't think we can bring 'er up far enough on the beach to keep 'er from drifting away. One rogue wave and we'd be marooned, sure we would." He glanced over to Pete. "Yeh did such a good job at the helm, Pirate Pete, d' yeh think yeh can take her out and anchor 'er if I abandon ship now?"

"I believe I can, sir," Pete said.

"After yeh drop the hook, yeh'll have t' swim t' shore," Mr. Heuck advised.

"Aye, Cap'n," Pete said. He was surprised to be singled out for the job. Besides, as hot as the day was becoming, a quick dip in Lake Huron would feel good.

"All right, step t' the wheel, Mis-ter Jenkins," Captain Heuck said, emphasizing the Mister. "The *Bing*'s in your hands." He looked at Dan and Kate. "Will yeh be jumpin' ship wi' me, er swimmin' t' shore with me first mate?"

Kate looked to her brother, who nodded. "We'll stay aboard with Mister Jenkins, sir," Kate said.

"Arghh, fair enough," Captain Heuck said. "Take her out thirty yards or so and drop anchor. We'll have some towels ready when yeh come ashore, we will. Oh, and yeh'd better give me yer boots and hose. I'll take 'em t' shore and keep 'em dry. Yeh wouldn't want t' be walkin' this 'ere rocky isle, searchin' fer buried treasure in bare feet, would yeh now? No, sure yeh wouldn't."

Dan, Kate and Pete each slipped out of their shoes and socks and handed them to the captain. "Take 'er for a little spin if ye like, but don't be long," he said as he moved forward and took a hand from Neal and Duke.

Pete pulled the *Bing*'s gear to reverse. He bumped the throttle forward, increasing the RPMs. The *Bing* moved slowly away from the island. He spun the wheel and pushed the gear forward, setting his sights on the open water. They had gone about twenty yards when Pete noticed that Dan's eyes were glued to a distant spot way off to port.

"Pete," Dan said. "Hand me Mr. Heuck's spyglass. It's in the box next to the wheel." There was no pirate lingo in Dan's speech. He sounded dead serious.

Pete found the telescope and passed it to Dan, then looked in the direction Dan was staring. "What's out there?"

"Not sure," Dan answered quietly. "It's no freighter, I can tell you that. I think it's a sailboat."

"A sailboat?" Pete asked. "What's so great about seeing a sailboat?"

There was a faraway softness in Dan's voice when he answered, "This is no ordinary sailboat."

Kate jumped to her brother's side. "Let me see,"

she insisted. Dan handed her the spyglass. She glanced quickly, then wiped the lens and peered through it again. A moment later she gasped, "It can't be." As she said this, a chilly breeze blew across the *Bing*'s deck, gripping the crew in a sudden shiver.

"It can't be what?" Pete asked anxiously. He felt the drop in temperature and noticed goose bumps rising on Kate's arms. In the next compartment was a yellow nylon jacket. He grabbed it and passed it to her.

"Thanks," Kate whispered as she put it on. "I don't know if it's the wind or what I see out there that has come over me."

"It's the wind," Pete said, trying to lighten her mood. "Come on, let me see."

Kate handed the spyglass to Pete. He peered into the distance. His jaw dropped. "What in the world?" he gasped. "I've never seen anything like it . . . except . . ." His voice trailed off.

"Except what?" Dan asked.

"Except last night," Pete completed softly. "It's just like the one in my dream."

The three stood at the *Bing*'s helm, staring for several minutes into the Lake Huron shipping channel. The engine kept chugging away from Gravelly Island as they watched the strange three-masted schooner approach.

"She's coming our way," Dan said. The three pirates no longer needed the spyglass to see the mysterious ship moving toward them.

"Let's go out and meet it!" Kate exclaimed. She zipped the yellow nylon jacket to her neck as if bracing herself, not only for the chilly breeze but also for a new adventure.

Pete could see that the schooner, with all its sails unfurled, was no more than half a mile away. "You're kidding, right?" he said. "Mr. Heuck told us to anchor the *Bing* and swim to shore. He didn't tell us to chase a boat around Lake Huron. I have to obey the captain!"

"He said you could take a little spin," Kate urged. "I heard him."

"She's coming fast," Dan said. "Come on, Pete. It will take just a few minutes. When the others at the party see us going out there, they'll be green with envy. We'll never get close to a boat like this again."

"Pete, hurry!" Kate prodded. "Ships like this have been gone from the Great Lakes for ages. Maybe we can get within range to salute her."

Pete had a choice. He could follow Mr. Heuck's orders and stay on the good side of the scariest man he'd ever seen, or he could listen to Kate. It was hardly a choice. He spun the *Bing*'s wheel and pushed the throttle to full speed. The old Navy lifeboat chugged away from Gravelly Island and directly into the path of the mysterious ship.

In changing direction, Pete also set himself on a course that would affect not only his day, but, as he would soon discover, his very existence.

46

CHAPTER 7
A DATE WITH DESTINY
12 JULY, 1812

Fifteen-year-old Will Drake, his father standing beside him, leaned against the passenger ship's railing. He gazed across the vast blue expanse at Bois Blanc Island off Michigan Territory's eastern shore. Beyond a narrow band of golden sand, a dense pine forest stretched as far as Will could see. The *Ticonderoga* was now only hours from Mackinac Harbor. The young traveler, tall, tanned and with long brown hair, looked very handsome in his new gentleman's clothes. Still, never having been this far from his home, he seemed a bit uneasy about life on the wild frontier.

If Detroit was any example, he was not expecting much. The little fort town, consisting of barely seven hundred souls, mostly American soldiers, merchants and farmers, comprised nothing more than a few small stores and some narrow, dirty streets. The riverside inn where his family had spent the night featured a noisy tavern, greasy food and a host of ill-mannered patrons. Mackinac Island, his father assured him, was an older, more civilized place. Will hoped so, for he knew the northern outpost was even farther removed from his native home.

Plans for the Drakes' trip had begun immediately after Will's dad had been promoted to a new position— chief comptroller of the American Fur Company. His duties would take his family to the remote village of Mackinac Island in the upper lakes. His dad's boss, John Jacob Astor, had given Mr. Drake a huge salary, but to

Will Drake

earn it he must take command of the backwoods outpost and establish complete control over the French-Canadian woodsmen, the various aboriginal tribes, and the British loyalists who lived among the American citizens. The position would require an iron fist on one hand and a delicate negotiating touch on the other, but the opportunity for great fortune was immense.

Mr. Drake had jumped at the chance. He quickly sold their home in New York and made arrangements to buy a new one on Mackinac Island. He placed the money netted from the sale of his property together with all his family's possessions in two huge trunks.

The family began the long journey by loading everything into an oxcart and setting off from New York City overland to Buffalo. Will found the roads on the western frontier were muddy and slow. Wagon wheels and axles broke and had to be repaired. After two weeks, Will and his parents made it to the shore of Lake Erie.

From there, they boarded the four-masted brig *Ticonderoga* and sailed west. The water route took a week before the ship landed in Detroit where the Drakes stayed the night. They reboarded the next morning for the final leg of the voyage to the northern tip of Lake Huron.

If the first half of the sail was not bad enough, the passage north from Detroit was an even more dangerous venture. On Lake Huron, gale-force winds buffeted the tall ship, nearly ripping sails from their shrouds. Then, for three days straight, the *Ticonderoga* sat totally becalmed, bobbing off Saginaw Bay like a balsam boat in a bathtub. The sun baked the sailors on deck. The stiffling air suffocated the passengers in their staterooms. Then, on the morning of the fourth day, with everyone aboard suffering miserably, a westerly breeze finally filled the *Ticonderoga*'s sails. To the whoops and cheers of passengers and sailors alike, the tall ship sped north.

Their destination nearly in sight, Will Drake stood with his father, Josiah Drake, leaning against the ship's railing. The July sun warmed the deck, but a cool breeze filled every inch of canvas, making the final day's sail a pleasant one.

As the two stood quietly watching the shoreline, Mr. Drake saw a look of concern on his son's face. He put his hand on Will's shoulder. "This will be a great adventure for you, Will," he said.

"I suppose," Will answered. "I look forward to living on the frontier, but I'm worried that war with England will begin soon. Fort Michilimackinac will surely be attacked."

Mr. Drake patted Will's arm. "Mr. Astor has hired me to do a job for the American Fur Company, not fight a war with Britain," he said soothingly. "Mr. Astor is a sharp businessman. I'm sure he has such affairs under control."

Will nodded, but he couldn't help thinking how his settled life in New York City had been turned upside down by his father's promotion. Activities with his old friends, his social life and his plans for college were all suddenly altered.

"Mr. Astor has offered us a great opportunity," Mr. Drake added. "He will soon control the entire fur trade. I will be his chief employee, and you will serve as my assistant."

"What will *I* do?" Will asked.

"You will be my representative to local merchants—my agent to Indians and Canadian trappers," Mr. Drake said. "You will be my goodwill ambassador. There are many British loyalists on Mackinac Island, and you will help make Mr. Astor's company visible to them all. Still, you will have time to fish, hunt and explore. Your friends back home will envy you your adventures."

"But why so far?" Will asked. "Why not somewhere nearer home?"

"Mackinac Island is the most strategic place in the entire Northwest," Mr. Drake said. "Any ship traveling through the upper lakes must pass within its view. For that reason, it is a critical military point. The United States will defend it with great vigor, which will serve Mr. Astor's needs as well. It is also the most convenient place in North America to collect the pelts that our agents bring from as far west as the Mississippi River and as far north as the frozen fields of Upper Canada."

Will turned to his father. "Other fur companies are already out here, some British, some American," he said. "What makes Mr. Astor think he can take over?"

Mr. Drake smiled. "Other companies insist the Indians travel great distances to their outposts with their pelts and then give inferior goods in trade. Mr. Astor's agents will go directly to the natives' villages and then trade better merchandise for the furs. It won't be long before all the agents will be working for Mr. Astor."

"Mr. Astor must know what he's doing," Will allowed.

Mr. Drake stood quietly, as if deciding how to state his next point. Finally, he said, "This all has been very difficult for your mother. As you know, she was born of British nobility. Her grandfather, Lord Pembroke, came to the Colonies years ago to manage his family's plantation in Virginia. By the time of the Revolution, he had passed away and his son, your grandfather, was in charge of the family's property. He was a friend of George Washington, Tom Jefferson, Jamie Madison and many another of our country's founding fathers. He fought the British governors who taxed the landowners without giving them any say in how they were governed. In fact, Mr. Pembroke had become quite the colonial rebel. He was so despised in England that, during the Revolution, a redcoat battalion burned his home. Your grandfather and grandmother were killed in that blaze, but somehow your mother escaped.

"At the time, I was a young private in George Washington's Continental Army. General Washington had sent me ahead of his troops to learn what the British were doing in the area. As I neared your mother's home, I saw smoke and hurried to it. I found her as she stumbled along the road, her clothes in rags. She told me that her parents were dead, murdered by the redcoats.

"I learned that she was 15 years old, the same as myself. In spite of her sad condition, she was the prettiest girl I'd ever seen. I was completely taken by her beauty. I would have carried her in my arms all the way to General Washington's camp if necessary. But when I took her hand to console her, she immediately straightened her back. 'Sir,' she said. 'I am not for the taking.'

" 'I assure you, ma'am,' I said, stepping back, 'I had no such intention. I'd only hoped to help.'

"She looked into my eyes and said, 'I see that now. I recognize by your uniform that you are a member of General Washington's army. He was my father's friend. Could you take me to him?'

" 'I would regard it an honor,' I told her. I reported back to General Washington, who recognized her and gave me permission to accompany her to her aunt's place in New York City."

Will had taken his eyes from the Bois Blanc Island shoreline and was now staring at his father. He had never heard this about his mother's childhood.

"And that is how your mother and I met," Josiah Drake continued. "After the war, I was released from my duties and traveled immediately to the place I had left her. By then, her aunt had died, and your mother was in the employ of a seamstress in a filthy sweatshop in the center of the city. She was still as beautiful as when I'd met her, but now penniless and boarding at the workhouse dormitory. With the money I'd earned from my service to the army, I was able to buy a modest house and we married.

"We have since very slowly become a family of means, small as they might be. The prospect of war with Britain once again looms large and weighs heavily on your mother's mind. Her experience with the redcoats left an indelible mark. Leaving the safety of the East Coast and moving to the wilderness is very hard for her. She will need our support as we deal with the various hardships on the frontier. I know that this has been difficult for you, too, leaving your school and friends, but it will be even harder for her."

Will turned from his father and again stared across the blue horizon. If his mother could survive her hardships without her parents, then surely he could learn to live in the frontier village with his. In some ways, Will actually looked forward to his new life. He just wished his family's destination could have been a little closer to home. Still, he pictured great hunting and fishing expeditions and meeting Indian boys and learning their ways. Life would be very different, but it would be rewarded with great adventures in the wild new world.

Caledonia

CHAPTER 8
A STRANGE SHIP APPROACHES

The *Ticonderoga* had almost reached the Straits of Mackinac. Bois Blanc Island was off her port bow, and the ship was cruising easily in a fair wind only thirty miles from her final destination.

As the four-masted ship cut silently through the rolling blue water, something ahead caught Will Drake's eye. A smaller, three-masted vessel was approaching. "Dad, that brig is cutting us off!" he said.

Mr. Drake tried to speak casually, but there was an odd catch in his voice. "Y-yes, I've been watching her. She . . . she appeared from around the northern end of Bois Blanc Island about two minutes ago—come to greet us, I suppose."

Will Drake assessed the wind's force and direction—also his father's hesitation. "But look! She's flying the Union Jack!"

"I'm sure everything's fine, son," Josiah Drake said, trying to sound reassuring. "The British have been stopping ships on the high seas, but they would not dare try it here on Lake Huron. We are clearly within American waters. They would be in direct violation of the Jay Treaty. I'm sure there's no cause for alarm. Some reasonable explanation will be forthcoming. Now, go below and tell your mother that there may be a momentary delay. Make it clear there is nothing to fear."

Will took one more look at the approaching ship and noticed that three gunports were now open, with a dozen men rolling cannon into position.

Will reached the stairway that led from the main deck to the companionway. He then darted along the hall to the passengers' cabins. In another moment he burst into his family's stateroom.

Mrs. Drake stood between two narrow, wooden beds. She was folding clothes into a trunk, which, within hours, would be unloaded from the ship and taken to their new home on Mackinac Island's Market Street. Smiling happily, she turned and faced Will. Noting his anxious expression, she asked, "What is it?"

"I'm not sure," the lanky fifteen-year-old said. "Father says it's nothing, but a British ship is approaching. It looks to have—"

Just then a tremendous blast thundered outside. Screams of terror came from above decks. The *Ticonderoga* rolled to port. After several moments, she righted herself. Then suddenly, she heeled to starboard. Inside the Drakes' small stateroom, two trunks slammed against the bulkhead.

Mrs. Drake was thrown off her feet. Will caught her arm, keeping her from striking her head against the wall. The two fell to the floor. The ship was listing badly.

"We must get up top!" Will yelled.

"We can't leave the trunks," his mother replied emphatically. She raised herself from the floor and grabbed a handle of the largest chest. She tugged with all her might to pull it away. It wouldn't budge. "Help me!" she shrieked.

Will ran to her side and took hold of the iron ring. With the ship tipping farther on its side, the trunk was wedged in solid. "Mother, forget the chests," Will implored. "We must make for the main deck!"

"But this is everything we own," she insisted. "I

can't start over again!"

Just then another resounding boom came from outside. A six-pound cannon ball smashed through the *Ticonderoga*'s hull and tore through the timbers of the Drakes' cabin. Water gushed in, sweeping a lantern from its hook. It smashed into the back of Mrs. Drake's head. Her beautiful face twisted into an expression of hopeless agony. Falling forward, she reached a hand toward Will, terror in her eyes and blood flowing freely from the wound. He lunged toward her, but she collapsed at his feet.

The cabin quickly flooded and Will was pressed against the door. He watched his mother's limp body sloshing, face up and eyes open. Thick, red blood surrounded her head. He fought his way to her and lifted her to her feet. He grabbed her arm, opened the door and pulled her through the rising torrent into the corridor.

Half-walking, half-swimming, he brought her through the darkness forward through the passageway. He looked ahead for light and then turned to see that his mother's face had drifted, once again, beneath the water's surface. He drew her toward him and stared into her lifeless blue eyes. He pressed his fingers to the side of her neck, praying to find a pulse. There was none. She was dead.

He could do nothing more. He kissed her, let go her arm, and watched her body drift down through the swirling current. She was swallowed up in the darkness of the sinking ship and taken from him forever. In the frigid water, Will felt a hot stream of tears pour down his cheeks.

Sorrow and rage quickly filled Will Drake's thoughts. He would avenge her death! Some how, some way, if it was the last thing he did, he would have revenge. But now, he had to get out of there.

He turned and fought his way toward the main deck. As he reached the hatch, a sudden torrent of water from below forced him through it, shooting him into brilliant sunshine and sweeping him yards away from the sinking ship. In the next moment, he found himself treading water. He turned and saw only the *Ticonderoga*'s portside railing above the surface. As he watched, the schooner groaned. A whoosh of air escaped and she disappeared.

Will struggled to tread water, but his clothes were pulling him under. He yanked off his boots and threw aside his heavy coat. The icy lake took his breath as he glanced about. Nearby, several uniformed sailors' bodies floated lifelessly, face-down. Will turned in all directions, hoping to find his father still alive. There, only twenty feet distant, a head bobbed to the surface, facing him. The man's eyes were set upon Will. It was his father! Pain and horror tortured his features, but he was alive! Will swam desperately toward him. As he did, he heard his father choke. Will watched as Mr. Drake inhaled a lungful of the deathly fluid and slipped, once again, beneath the surface.

Will dived. Pulling with his arms and kicking frantically, he peered through the turbid water. Directly in front of him but beyond Will's reach, he saw his father's form sinking rapidly into the depths. Still, he kicked and stroked downward, but in the deepening darkness, his father disappeared. Will would never see him again—except in the nightmares that would torment him for the rest of his life. His chest exploding in pain, Will turned, pulling and kicking until he finally broke the surface.

Gasping for air, he stared in the direction of his drowned father. As he did, something hard landed on the top of his head. He grabbed the object. It was a thick rope. He pulled it, turning himself around. He found himself facing the enemy ship. A man in a red jacket stood aboard the British vessel, holding the other end of the line. Will tugged angrily, trying to jerk the soldier into the water, but succeeded only in drawing himself closer to his grinning foe.

"Here, fishy, fishy," the man taunted with a squeaky voice. He reeled Will in like a played-out mackerel. "Come aboard and meet Mr. Moneypenny! He'll want his deck cleaned after hauling in the filthy likes of you."

"You can't do this!" Will screamed. "You have no right to attack our ship."

"On the contrary," the man replied with a high-pitched snort. "We have every right in the world."

CHAPTER 9
WILL BOARDS THE *CALEDONIA*

Arnold Skaggs dragged Will Drake to the British ship's railing and dropped a boarding ladder over the side. Will grabbed the lowest rung and drew himself up to the soldier, who grinned mockingly above. Shaking with cold, fear and rage, Will crawled onto the deck and stood to face his captor. The man was wearing a soldier's red coat with blue trim, white pants, crimson sash and tall gaiters. Two white belts crossed his chest, one holding a cartridge box, the other sheathing a bayonet. The soldier's stovepipe cap made him look tall, but Will knew he had him by at least four inches and maybe twenty pounds.

The soldier's jaw was weak, and he had tiny, red-rimmed, pale gray eyes. His pointed teeth were crooked and badly discolored. In all, he resembled a diseased rat.

The small man circled Will, appraising his catch. "You're not much," he chirped, "but I guess you'll have to do. I am Sergeant Skaggs and you are my prisoner."

"I'm an American!" Will protested angrily.

"Not anymore," Skaggs said. "You are a traitor to the Crown and a disgrace to your English heritage. If you have any sense at all, you will do exactly as you're told. I am here aboard the *Caledonia* as General Isaac Brock's personal emissary. Come with me. I'm taking you to Mr. Moneypenny, the ship's captain. Although he is not a military man as I am, you will answer to him. Since the *Caledonia* is sailing somewhat shorthanded, you'll be put to work in the service of the King, just like the rest

Sergeant
Arnold Skaggs

of the crew."

"You can't do this!" Will argued. "This ship is in American waters, and you are in violation of the Jay Treaty."

"Not anymore we're not." The Englishman chortled as he drew his bayonet from its sheath. He pointed it into Will's chest and motioned him toward the quarterdeck. "Go!"

A cold, dazed and angry Will Drake followed the little man's orders and moved up a half flight of stairs. From there, they went aft to the ship's helm. Skaggs approached an elderly man standing at the wheel. The man wore a nautical uniform, but it was not that of a British naval officer. His attire was more that of a merchant seaman. Still, his square features, confident bearing and wizened countenance marked him as master of the ship.

"Mr. Moneypenny," Skaggs said, "I'm sorry to report that this boy is the only survivor from the American vessel. He says he was a passenger, if you can believe a Yank. Unfortunately, we were unable to bring any useful seamen aboard, as she went down almost immediately."

Mr. Moneypenny stared indifferently at Will. "What business was it that brought you west?"

"I am . . . *was* with my parents," Will said, his voice rising. He bit his upper lip, trying to conceal his anger. He'd always been good at hiding emotions, but now that his whole life had been turned upside down, his lip trembled and his breaths came in short gasps. "We . . . we were going to Mackinac Island. My father was to be Mr. Astor's chief agent for the American Fur Company."

"And they perished in the battle?" Mr. Moneypenny asked casually.

Will became incensed at the man's callousness.

"Battle, sir! What battle?" he shouted, "You just murdered an entire shipload of people! How do you explain that?"

Mr. Moneypenny turned and faced the new conscript. "We are at war, son," he said firmly. "If you were not aware, it was declared by your President Madison a month ago. I am sorry about your parents, but you now must understand your place. I will give you a choice. You will either become a member of this ship's crew and serve the King, or you will be kept below as a prisoner of war. If you are wise, you will choose the former and be fed, clothed and sheltered just as any other sailor aboard the *Caledonia*. Choose the latter and you will take permanent residence in the ship's brig, a very unpleasant alternative, I can assure you. Is that clear?"

"I will never serve your tyrant King!" Will stormed.

"As you please," Moneypenny said. "You may wish to reconsider after a night or two below." He turned to Skaggs. "Take our prisoner to the bilge and place him in irons. We'll see how long it takes before his insolence is tempered by reason."

"Aye, Captain," Skaggs said with a sneer. He grabbed Will by the arm and pushed him away from the helm. He shoved his bayonet's point against Will's back.

As Will marched away, he saw Moneypenny raise a small megaphone to his mouth. "Hoist all sail and make for St. Joseph's Island!" he ordered.

His command was relayed to the various officers who immediately barked their instructions to the other seamen. There was a general echoing of directives on down the chain of command until Will could not look in any direction without seeing sailors moving through the crosstrees and along the deck, high and low from stem to stern. Lines were being laid, halyards drawn, sails raised and ropes belayed. Will quickly realized that when the captain spoke, everyone jumped. He vowed that *he* would not!

From the main deck, Skaggs opened a hatch and directed Will down a stairway. They didn't stop there but continued through narrower and steeper passages deeper into the bowels of the ship. Each landing was smaller and darker than the one before. Finally, Will descended a short ladder to the very bottom of the vessel. The soldier opened a small door and sent Will sprawling into a cell no bigger than a casket. Putrid water sloshed across the roughly hewn plank hull. The jailor clamped rusty manacles to Will's hands and feet, leaving him lying hunched over and unable to straighten his legs or back. Then, with a derisive snort, Skaggs slammed and bolted the door.

The room was black. Will was wet, cold and miserable. When he could no longer hear the soldier's footsteps, he felt a knot in his throat. Thoughts of the past hour flooded his mind—cannonballs blasting the *Ticonderoga*'s hull, the iron lantern smashing his mother's skull, feeling the chilling cold of Lake Huron's depths, his father's final terrified expression, and now tasting this bilge cell's putrid water. Each thought stabbed Will like a dagger and gripped him with utter despair. All hope was lost. Will cried—openly cried— like a baby.

The ship rocked relentlessly as it plowed ahead. With each wave, bilge water splattered his face. He imagined it rising, and soon he would be chained beneath it, gasping desperately until his final breath would drown him. The force of the waves striking the hull caused his head to crash time and again against the cell wall. He was so bitterly cold and in such agony that even with all that had happened in the last hour, he could not think of anything but the intolerable pain. With one particularly large wave, his head smashed against an iron bolt. He slumped into unconsciousness.

When he came to, it was like awakening from a nightmare. At first, he imagined he was home in his own bed, but his forehead throbbed and his body ached all over. He was unbearably hot. He tried to rub his eyes, but something held his hands from his face. He blinked, but his bedroom was as black as a tomb. Suddenly, it all flashed before him. He rolled from side to side, agonizing over the enormity of his fate.

Then, along with his other miseries, Will felt a sharp pain at the tip of his left big toe. He kicked and struck something hard but furry. An animal scurried over his legs, then up to his chest. Its sharp claws dug into his skin as it crept slowly over his chin to his mouth, over his nose, eyes and forehead. Will shook convulsively and the creature scrambled away through an unseen hole in the ship's chamber of horrors.

"Let me out of here!" Will shrieked. Nobody answered. He yelled again and again until his breath ran out. He fell back, exhausted. After several minutes, he heard footsteps along the corridor.

"What do you want?" Arnold Skaggs chirped. Will was actually glad to hear the weasel's squeaky voice.

"I'm being eaten alive," Will hollered.

"Rats get hungry too," the British soldier taunted. "Mr. Moneypenny will see you—maybe tomorrow."

"I'll be dead by then!" Will said, pleading.

"It is nothing to me," the guard replied. "My orders are to keep you here until the captain says. Wake me up once more and I may sleep through his call." Skaggs turned and marched up to the next deck.

Will was now wide awake. He was more scared than ever before in his life. Lying in his cell, he took account of his situation. He had one chance and one chance only to get out of this cell. He'd have to stand before Moneypenny, the man who had ordered the attack on the *Ticonderoga*, and beg for mercy. Will had no choice: he would accept any terms the captain offered. Staying locked in this rat-infested hole would come to no good. Once on deck, Will might find a way to escape—and perhaps avenge his parents' deaths.

He felt his stomach cramp with hunger. The airless cell was spinning. He fell back into unconsciousness.

-     -   -   -   -

A key clanked in the lock awakening Will. The door flew open, and a brilliant light blinded him.

"There you are, Mr. Drake." The sarcastic greeting was followed by a haughty laugh. It was Skaggs. "The captain will see you now. You owe me for this."

Will nodded without hesitation. "Yes, sir," he replied.

"You'd better behave," Skaggs warned, "or you'll rot in this cell with the key rusting at the bottom of Lake Huron." The soldier reached down and unlocked the chains, releasing Will's hands and feet. Skaggs drew his bayonet and jabbed it against Will's chest. "Follow me," he snarled.

Will rolled from the bilge cell and crawled through its tiny door. He stood hunched over in the low passageway. He knew that whatever it took, he never wanted to see this hellhole again.

CHAPTER 10
CALEDONIA SAILS TO ST. JOSEPH'S ISLAND

Will followed Arnold Skaggs up several levels of stairs and then marched from the bow to the captain's quarters at the very stern. Skaggs knocked at Mr. Moneypenny's door.

"What is it?" came the gruff response from within.

"It's Sergeant Skaggs, sir. The Yank is here."

"Let him in," Moneypenny said. Skaggs opened the door and Will stepped into the captain's spacious cabin. A quick glance at the bed, tables and chests told Will that this was the master's living, dining and office quarters. "You may be excused, Skaggs," Moneypenny said from his desk in the middle of the room. "Remain in the hall until I summon you." The soldier closed the door, and Will stood facing the ship's master.

"I hope a good night's sleep has improved your manners, Mr. Drake," Moneypenny said, eyeing his captive.

Will looked like anything but a person who'd had a good night's sleep. His normally well-groomed, long brown hair was snarled and dirty. His living tomb had alternately frozen him at night and boiled him like a lobster during the hot July day. His face, hands and legs were slimy from rolling in bilge water. His sweat-streaked brow bore cuts and bruises from banging against the ship's hull. His knickers and shirt—all that remained of his best clothes—were torn and ruined. His bare feet were bloody from rat bites, and his wrists and ankles were chafed raw from the rusty manacles. He could barely stand from having spent the night

69

hunched over in irons. He was physically and emotionally bankrupt.

Still, as he stood before the man who had ordered the attack that had killed his parents, he remembered Skaggs' warning. He would get one chance to keep from lodging permanently in the ship's bilge. He quickly responded, "Yes, sir."

"Are you prepared to behave as a loyal British seaman and obey your superiors' commands?" Moneypenny's words were not a question but an order.

"I will, sir," Will answered. With only a moment's hesitation he added, "There is something I don't understand."

Moneypenny looked up in surprise. He was not used to being questioned—certainly not by a pressed sailor. In a flash of remembrance, Moneypenny recalled the deaths of his own parents at the hands of a band of pirates off the Ivory Coast. He had been no more than a boy himself at the time. Considering the circumstances of Will Drake's parents' fate, he responded more kindly than he might otherwise have. "And what is that?"

"This *is* a merchant ship, right?" Will asked.

"In peacetime, yes," the captain answered. "The *Caledonia* is owned by the North West Fur Company."

"Then why did you sink the *Ticonderoga?*"

The captain stiffened and his eyes bore into those of the boy before him. "You're sailing mighty close to the wind, young man," he said. Then his expression changed. He paused and sat back in his chair. "Ordinarily, Mr. Drake, I would not submit to such an inquiry, but under the circumstances, I feel a brief explanation would not be out of order. In times of war, the King may bid his subjects to perform for the common good of the country. A week ago, General

70

Captain Moneypenny

Brock asked me to deliver a message. He also ordered me to capture or sink any American ship that I might find along the way."

"But my parents didn't know anything about the war," Will said.

"My instructions were clear," Moneypenny responded tersely. He looked to be at the end of his patience, but still he went on, "I would liked to have captured the *Ticonderoga* and made it a British vessel, but its great size prohibited that. Its American crew would have outnumbered mine; mutiny would have been inevitable. War is a time for following instructions. Had I not sunk your ship, I would have been tried in a British court and hanged for treason.

"I am truly sorry about your parents, and I will do everything in my power to see that you are treated fairly aboard this ship, but I must have your word that you will follow commands."

Will Drake's upper lip trembled. "Yes, sir," he said finally.

"Henceforth, you will be my cabin boy," Moneypenny said. "You will take care of my quarters and perform other such duties as I shall assign. Skaggs will have charge over you as his prisoner, but I, as ship's captain, have some control over him. He fears you may cause trouble if you are given full rights of a seaman, so he has insisted that you be contained at night in the ship's bow, quartered in an empty sail locker. See to it that you do not violate my trust." Mr. Moneypenny stood and offered his right hand.

Will stepped forward and accepted it. "Yes, sir," he said with a nod.

The captain moved to the door. Opening it, he spoke to the British soldier. "Sergeant Skaggs, you will take

Mr. Drake to the ship's store and have him outfitted in proper sailor's clothes. See that he is issued a hammock and blankets. You will then take him to his new quarters. You are excused."

"Aye, Captain," Skaggs said with a salute. He turned and squeezed Will's shoulder—hard. He shoved his prisoner along the walkway. "I have some plans for you," he snarled.

"What plans are those?" Will asked.

"You'll learn soon enough, *boy*," Skaggs said harshly. "You will begin by addressing me with respect! Henceforth, you will speak only when I question you, and then you will address me as 'Sergeant Skaggs, *sir*!' Otherwise, you will keep your Yankee trap shut!"

Will stared blankly at his keeper. As the moments passed, anger began to show on the soldier's face. His cheeks and neck flushed and then turned a shade of crimson. "You have been spoken to by a *superior*!" Skaggs screamed. "*Speak* when you are spoken to!"

Will calmly responded, "I was not aware you had asked a question."

Skaggs flew into a rage. "*Sir!*" He screamed. "Call me 'Sir,' or . . . or I'll . . . I'll . . . I'll *kill* you!" He fumbled with his bayonet, but in his frenzy, he was unable to withdraw it from its sheath.

Will stood calmly as Arnold Skaggs became nearly apoplectic with fury. Clearly, the soldier could not control himself in times of stress.

Finally, Will replied casually, "Yes, *sir*, Sergeant Skaggs, *sir*!" Will knew he had one small advantage over his captor. He just had to find the right time to use it.

Arnold Skaggs' normal waxy color slowly returned to his face. "That's better," he said. "Now, to the ship's store with you. Make haste."

Down one more flight of stairs they went and into
a room crammed with supplies. "We have a new recruit,
Farnsworth," Skaggs said brusquely to the man at the
desk. The elderly man's right arm was missing at
the elbow.

"Who you got here, Arnold?" the ship's purser asked,
sizing up the new sailor.

"Nobody much," Skaggs said. "Just a Yankee boy
who's forgotten his allegiance to his home country. I
picked him out of the water back there off Bois Blanc.
Skipper wants him fitted out for service. He needs
all the able-bodied seamen he can get—enlisted
or pressed."

"We'll just start a tab for you, young man," the
storekeeper said. "You'll work it off as we sail. Let's
see, you look to be about five-foot-nine and eleven
stone," he said, estimating Will's height and weight.
"This jacket, blouse and trousers should do. And these
shoes and hose will make you into a proper sailor—in
appearance, at least. What's your name, son?"

"Drake, sir. Will Drake."

Farnsworth pulled a small ledger marked "Accounts
Book" from his vest pocket and set it on the desk. He
opened it and found his most recent entry. He dipped
his quill into an ink pot and, at the bottom of the page,
scrawled:

14 July, 1812
Lake Huron between Bois Blanc and St. Mary's River
W. Drake   Sailor's slops,   4s 6d   shoes & hose 1d

It was slow work for the one-armed man, but when
he was done, he looked at Will and smiled. "Used to be
right handed," Farnsworth said. "Lost it in the rigging

during a storm."

Will nodded.

"But I'm mighty obliged to the captain for keeping me aboard an' findin' me work." He reached back and withdrew a rope net and two blankets from a shelf. "You'll need these, too," he said. "Gets a mite chilly at night." He added to the ledger,

bedding loaned

Will took his new clothes, hammock and blankets and turned to the door. Once again, Skaggs pushed him along the ship's corridors. They came to an empty room one deck below the crew's quarters in the ship's forecastle, or fo'c's'le, as Skaggs called it. The soldier unlocked the door and pointed to some hooks at each end of the small room. "Hang your hammock there," he ordered. "This is your new home. If you cross me, it's back to the bilge—irons, rats and all. Keep on my good side, if you know what's best for you. Now, get into yer slops!"

Will removed his ruined clothes. He donned the red-and-white-striped shirt, white pants, blue jacket and neckerchief. He pulled the long white stockings up to his knees and slipped his feet into the shoes. A black, narrow-brimmed hat completed the uniform. He stared down at himself and suddenly felt sick. He looked like any other British sailor aboard. Still, his new clothes were warm and dry, and for that he was grateful. Just now, he'd do what he had to do to survive, but somehow he would get revenge.

Skaggs opened the locker door and pushed Will into the passageway.

"Where are you taking me?" Will asked.

"*Sir!*" Arnold Skaggs squeaked. His face became contorted and crimson. "You will call me 'Sergeant Skaggs, *sir*'! Understood? I'll have you back in your cell with rats gnawing on your hide if you don't mind your tongue!"

"Sorry, sir," Will responded quickly, "but the captain told me to return to him to be his cabin boy."

"He *what?*" Skaggs' face again turned an awful shade of red. "*I'll* tell you what you're doing. Now, move ahead! You will swab the deck and whistle 'God Save the King' whilst doing it!"

CHAPTER 11
THE *CALEDONIA* CAPTURES
A STRANGE VESSEL

For the next several hours, Skaggs kept Will Drake busy far from Mr. Moneypenny's view. Beginning at the ship's lowest level, Will swabbed the *Caledonia*'s decks. Eventually, with Skaggs always nearby, Will moved up to the quarterdeck, where the captain commanded the ship.

There, Will started scrubbing at the stern, out of the captain's sight. He was on his hands and knees when he looked over the port railing. He noticed that the *Caledonia* was approaching some islands and was about to pass very close to one. This might be his chance for freedom! With Skaggs not looking, Will could jump from the deck and swim to shore. His fate on these uninhabited islands would be no worse than serving the enemy for the rest of his life. Closer and closer the *Caledonia* sailed to the green point of land.

As Will considered his options, he saw, coming from the island, a small, gray, canoe-shaped boat. What was thoroughly odd was that it proceeded on an upwind course without benefit of sail. Nor did the three strangely attired people aboard use paddles or oars to propel their craft. Will then noticed, upon a closer look, that only *two* of the three wore unusual clothes. The third was dressed exactly as he was—another merchant sailor, no doubt.

Will looked around to see if Skaggs or anyone else was aware of this peculiar vessel. It appeared that none were, and the three strangers continued their approach.

77

By then, the boat had slipped close behind the *Caledonia*. As it neared, Will heard a faint *chug-chug-chug* sound coming from the mysterious craft. He stared in amazement and debated whether he should cast his fate with such an eerie apparition or stay in the relative safety of his prison ship.

Just then a blond-haired fellow in the gray boat waved and smiled excitedly, calling, "Ahoy! Who goes there?"

-     -   -   -   -

Dan Hinken stood with his hands still cupped to his mouth after hailing the tall ship. Kate stared excitedly at the marvelous reproduction. The *Bing,* now only thirty feet from its stern, was growing dangerously close to ramming it. Pete pulled back on the throttle, keeping the *Bing* at a safe distance.

As he did, he noticed a strange sensation coming from his jacket. He reached into the vest and felt the accounts book. It was warm!

As Pete gazed at the old schooner, he saw a sailor on the top deck staring down at them. The long-haired fellow seemed anxious—even scared.

-     -   -   -   -

Will Drake glanced over his shoulder. He could not call down to the friendly faces below for fear Skaggs would hear him. Instead, he put his finger to his lips to signal silence. His original plan to swim to the nearby islands was quickly amended to jumping ship and joining these strange people in their mysterious boat. He would do no worse with them, no matter who or what they were, than by staying aboard the *Caledonia*

Dan hailing the *Caledonia*

and serving the enemy.

Just then, Skaggs turned and noticed Will motioning-—as if to someone behind the ship. He next saw his prisoner raise his right leg to the railing. The Yank was going to jump overboard! Skaggs ran to him and grabbed his shoulder. Will lost his balance and tumbled back, slamming his head against the deck. He rolled another twenty feet before coming to rest against a stanchion. Skaggs then peered over the ship's stern and saw a small, gray boat with three people aboard. He whirled and yelled toward the *Caledonia*'s helm, "Captain! Come quick!"

Moneypenny turned and noted Skaggs' frantic expression. He ordered his first mate to take the wheel and then hurried to Skaggs' side. He gazed in wonder at the strange boat with its three passengers. One of them was Will Drake, the same lad who, only a few hours before, had pledged to serve the King and work dutifully as the ship's cabin boy.

"The prisoner was attempting an escape," Skaggs shouted.

"I can see that, Skaggs," Moneypenny growled. He put a megaphone to his mouth. "All hands on deck! Call out the watch!" He then scanned the horizon, looking for more enemy vessels. Seeing none, he turned to his crew and ordered, "Prepare the guns!"

There was a flurry of activity as twenty sailors scurried to positions all over the upper deck. In moments the *Caledonia* had slowed to a stop.

-    -   -   -   -

Pete, Dan and Kate looked eagerly at the perfectly reconstructed 19th century replica schooner. "Talk about

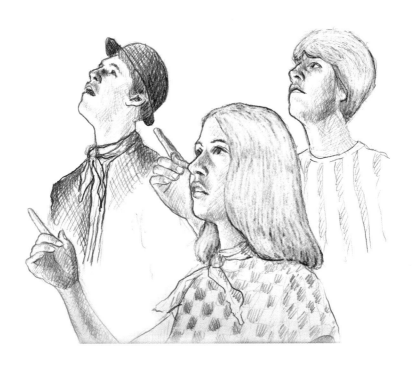

Pete, Dan And Kate
Looking Up At The Large Ship

luck!" Dan said. "We come out here to get a close look at an old ship and she stops for us. Can you believe it?"

"If we play our cards right, we might even be invited aboard!" Kate said. "Let's anchor here and have a visit."

"I wonder what happened to the first guy," Pete said. "I thought he was about to jump over the side when that soldier-guy grabbed him."

Just then, Mr. Moneypenny leaned over the railing, a pistol in his right hand. He looked into the canoe at three people, among them Will Drake, who had somehow, in the short time since he had last seen him, gotten a haircut.

"Young man!" Moneypenny yelled, pointing his pistol between Pete's eyes. "Do you know what you're doing? To attempt escape is treason! Who are your accomplices?"

Pete stood unblinking, his mouth wide open. The man seemed to be speaking to *him*! From the corner of his eye, Pete noticed three wooden doors opening along the ship's side. Men were rolling heavy cannon into place—all aimed directly at the *Bing*.

"Give up your vessel or we will fire!" shouted the captain. He was still staring at Pete.

With her dazzling smile and perky voice, Kate broke the tension. "Oh, come now," she said with a laugh. "We just came to say hi."

"Then what are you doing with my prisoner?" the man said, still aiming his pistol at Pete.

Pete nervously moved next to Dan and whispered, "This is a joke, right?"

"Cast your anchor at once!" Moneypenny shouted from above.

"Thank you, sir," Kate chirped happily. "We were just

about to do that."

"He looks serious," Pete said to Kate. "What's going on?"

"Beats me," Kate whispered, still smiling at the captain, "but I believe he's inviting us aboard. What a terrific stroke of luck! Besides, I think I know who's behind it."

"Who?" Pete asked as Kate tossed the *Bing*'s anchor over the side.

"Who else?" Dan whispered. "It's got to be Mr. Heuck. Let's just go along with it. This could be fun."

In the next moment two uniformed sailors lowered a rope ladder from the antique ship's quarterdeck.

"Climb aboard and be quick about it," the officer ordered.

In moments, Pete, Dan and Kate scaled the rope and stood on the deck surrounded by the *Caledonia*'s captain and crew.

Kate stepped toward the man in charge.

"So, who are you guys?" she asked pleasantly.

"You and your vessel are now under the command of His Royal Highness, King George III, under conditions of war," Moneypenny proclaimed. "You will submit to my orders or be held as prisoners in our ship's jail." He turned to a man at his side. "Skaggs, I thought you were watching the American! How did he get away?"

"He's right there," Skaggs defended, pointing off to the side. Will Drake was still woozy from his collision with the deck. He got to his feet and staggered to Skaggs' side.

Mr. Moneypenny turned first to Will Drake and then back to Pete Jenkins. "They're twins!" he said in surprise. He pointed to Will. "Go to your quarters. I will deal with you later."

Pete stared at his look-alike British sailor. Will gazed woozily at his mirror image. "Aye, sir," Will said. He turned and walked unsteadily to the stairway leading to the lower deck.

Moneypenny glared at Dan, Kate and Pete. "Judging by the waters we are sailing in, I would expect you are Americans. Is that right?"

Smiling sweetly, Kate spoke up, "That's right, sir. And you would be . . . ?"

"I would be Mr. Moneypenny, master of this ship and loyal subject to the King. And what, young lady, are you doing gallivanting about with bared arms and legs?"

"Excuse me?" Kate asked, confused by the man's question.

"You must know that it is not proper for a young lady to be seen in public dressed so . . . sparingly," Moneypenny said.

"Right," Kate said with an incredulous laugh.

"But back to the point," the captain continued, glancing at all three of the new prisoners. "I will offer you the same conditions I made the young American you have just seen. You may either remain in our brig in chains for the duration of our sail, or you may join our forces and become members of His Majesty's crew."

Kate smiled sweetly. "May we have a moment to discuss this?" she asked casually.

The captain studied the three for a moment, then answered, "You may have one minute."

Kate turned to Dan and Pete. Dan spoke first. "Whoever set this up has gone to great lengths to make it look real," he said. "Even the 'captain' here thinks he can toss us into his jail."

"I'm sure he's just an overeager history buff,

probably from some Great Lakes museum or other," Kate said. "But let's just say he intends to carry out his charade. I'd rather not waste whatever time we have aboard in a guest stateroom. I'd rather pretend we were crew and climb all over the ship. How about you, Pete?"

"I've got a really bad feeling about this," Pete said, again noting the warmth coming from his jacket pocket. "But I really don't like the 'jail in irons' idea."

Dan shook his head. His historical knowledge of the Great Lakes made him question the whole scenario. "There's something terribly wrong here. A ship like this hasn't been on the Lakes for years," he muttered. "And I'm sure I'd have heard about someone building such a perfect replica. Articles would have been in all the boating magazines."

Kate considered her brother's words. She then turned back to the captain. "We accept your kind invitation and would love to serve as members of your crew," she said pleasantly.

"So be it," Moneypenny said. He seemed puzzled by her cheerful demeanor. "You will take an oath of allegiance to the King. Raise your right hand."

"Sure," Kate said with a nod. She stepped forward, leaving Dan and Pete behind her. She raised her right hand and placed her left hand behind her back, crossing her fingers. Pete smiled inwardly at Kate's brilliance. He and Dan did the same.

Moneypenny glared skeptically at the three newcomers. "Do you hereby accept the King of England to be your sovereign master and, upon failing any responsibility to him, do willingly accept death as your penalty? If so, say, 'I will.' "

"I will," the three answered, each suppressing a grin.

Moneypenny turned to Skaggs. "Sergeant, take these

Kate Takes An Oath

recruits away and fit them out for service! And get this girl some proper clothes!"

"Aye, sir," Skaggs said. He turned to his three new prisoners and squeaked, "Follow me." As he led the three along the quarterdeck, he said over his shoulder, "You did the smart thing. His Majesty's troops will surely put down the American insurrection this time. You only won your little revolution because King George had more important concerns back on the Continent. The colonies will fall apart soon enough and come crawling back to Mother England."

As the three followed their loudmouth escort, Dan whispered to Kate and Pete. "Do any of these people relax?"

"This little twit certainly doesn't," Kate answered. "He seems to have fallen in love with his redcoat soldier role, don't you think?"

"Yeah," Dan replied. "Mr. Heuck has outdone himself this time."

"You're right," Kate agreed. "Probably all the other kids were in on it, too. That's why Mr. Heuck asked us to take the *Bing* out to anchor. He knew we'd see this boat and go out to it. He figured he'd give us a real adventure."

"Seems a little odd, though," Dan said, looking around. "A fully rigged, 19th-century brig—complete with captain and crew—that's a bit much, even for Mr. Heuck."

"And the man posing as the ship's captain is mighty convincing," Pete added. "British accent and all."

Kate laughed. "Don't be ridiculous," she said. "Mr. Heuck is perfectly capable of cooking this up. Since he's gone to all the bother, we might as well have fun with it."

"I guess you're right," Dan finally agreed. "It's the only answer."

As Pete followed the others, he tried to piece together a reasonable explanation for all of this—including the warmth coming from the book in his pocket. A nagging thought kept popping into his head.

The four descended a ladder to the main deck and walked its length to the bow before Skaggs opened a hatch and ordered them down another flight of stairs.

Kate ran ahead and tapped the man on the shoulder. "So, um, Mr. Skaggs," she called out pleasantly.

The British soldier spun on his heels. "It's 'Sergeant Skaggs!' " he shouted.

"Oh, yes. Right, right, right," Kate said with false seriousness. "A thousand pardons, Sergeant Skaggs. Anyway, you seem to have the captain's ear. What's he going to do—make us walk the plank?" At that, she shuddered dramatically. Dan couldn't contain himself, letting go a muffled snicker.

"You will not be making light when I inform the captain of your impudence," Skaggs squeaked, his face now turning from red to blue.

"Oh, now, Kate," Dan said mockingly, "we mustn't be so impudent." Unable to hold back, he broke out with a belly laugh.

As Skaggs glowered at the three new conscripts, a vein nearly popped in his neck. "You . . . you little Yankee pests! I'm going to tell the captain!" He took his eyes from Dan and Kate and noticed that the third prisoner was the only one who seemed to be taking him seriously. He pulled his bayonet from its sheath and pointed it at Pete's chest. "You, there!" he snarled. "March ahead. And if you don't, I'll . . . I'll spear you like a herring and toss you overboard." The long blade seemed to bolster the small man's confidence.

For the second time in one afternoon, first with Moneypenny aiming a pistol down at the *Bing* from the *Caledonia* and now with this British soldier-guy holding the business end of a very authentic-looking antique blade to his chest, blood drained from Pete's face.

With Pete looking so scared, Skaggs calmed to the point that he could speak. "I'm going to let you three have some time alone with your American friend. You'd better listen to him. He's had a night in the ship's brig, which is just where you'll be heading if you don't straighten up." Skaggs pushed the three along the darkening corridor until they approached Will Drake, who stood at the door outside his locked cell.

Pete noticed that Will was dressed in a uniform exactly like his, except that the longer-haired sailor was wearing socks and shoes just like the ones he had taken off and given to Mr. Heuck for safekeeping back at Gravelly Island. Other than that, the two were as alike in size and build as any two people could be. Their complexion and their facial features—even their hair, except for its length—were remarkably similar.

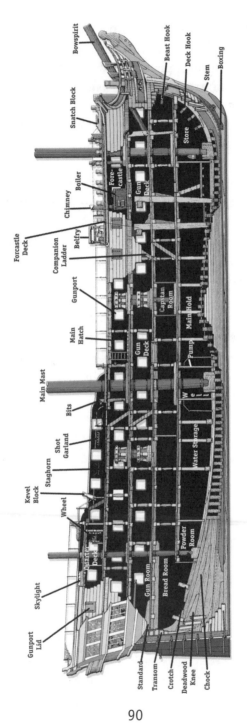

Schematic of the *Caledonia*

CHAPTER 12
A MEETING OF MINDS

The four Americans stood together at the door facing Skaggs. "I don't believe you have taken your oath to King George seriously," he squeaked. "I will give you some time with your Yankee friend to consider the consequences of high treason!" He took a key from his pocket, undid the lock and shoved all four into the bow compartment. He slammed the door and snapped the padlock behind him.

The room was smaller than a horse stall—and smelled no better. Two portholes looked out from the ship just above the *Caledonia*'s waterline. Almost no light or air passed into the tiny room. The three friends stared for several moments at the new boy. Finally, Kate said with a twinge of frustration, "All right. Who *are* you?"

"I am an American," Will replied, "and like you, a captive of the British Crown."

"Come on," Dan said with a scornful laugh. "We know this is all play-acting. Who put you up to this?"

Will seemed puzzled by Dan's accusing tone. Still, he responded sincerely, "I guess you could say Mr. Moneypenny. Until yesterday, I didn't know that England and the United States were at war. You're probably in the same situation as I was."

"And what situation is that?" Dan asked coldly. He sounded annoyed that yet another history geek would continue this maddening farce.

Will shrugged and answered, "One of involuntary servitude to the King, of course," he said.

Dan and Kate exchanged ironic smirks, but everything

seemed way too real to Pete. The pieces added up to something so impossible that he still couldn't make himself believe it.

Will Drake noticed Dan and Kate's suspicious expressions and decided he should tell them everything. "Yesterday morning," he began, "I was with my parents sailing to Michilimackinac. This British ship, the *Caledonia*, approached our boat and, with no warning, opened fire. A cannonball blasted a hole through our hull, and the *Ticonderoga* foundered at once. I was with my mother in our stateroom when a second ball tore through our cabin wall. It opened a huge hole just below the waterline next to where she stood."

Will remained silent for a moment. His eyes began to swell with tears. "She . . . my mom . . . was killed instantly. I tried to save her, but water flooded our room. I had to get up top or I'd have drowned right then. I made it to the main deck and was swept overboard. In the open water, I saw my father trying to stay afloat. He went down before I could get to him. Sergeant Skaggs, the British soldier you just met, threw a line and dragged me aboard. It was only then that I learned that the United States and Britain were at war. Skaggs chained me in a rat-infested cell where I stayed until this morning. I was scrubbing the decks when I saw you in that strange little boat of yours."

Dan still looked unconvinced, but Kate appeared stunned by their new acquaintance's horrific tale. Will Drake was either staging an Academy Award performance or telling the Gospel truth. There was no middle ground.

Pete also gaped. The sailor's story was beginning to sound very familiar—one that could only lead to an impossible conclusion.

As the three stared, keys rattled in the lock. The door

flew open, and Skaggs stood in the corridor, glaring at his charges. "Your time is up! How will you have it?" he demanded. "Will it be the bilge cell and its rats, or will you take your oath seriously?"

For once, Kate and Dan were lost for words. Pete stepped forward. "We want to be members of the crew," he said flatly.

"Then come with me," Skaggs ordered. He turned to Will. "I'll lead your fellow conscripts to the ship's store. You will follow them. Be sure they do not dawdle, Mr. Drake."

As he said this, Pete's head jerked up. Skaggs had called their new friend "Mr. Drake!" The reality hit him like a sailboat's boom. All the pieces fell together. He gawked at the fourth American.

"Aye, sir," Will replied. Skaggs backed into the passageway and signaled the others to follow.

When Skaggs had moved sufficiently ahead, Pete worked his way to Will's side. He nudged Dan and Kate, keeping them nearby. "Skaggs called you 'Mr. Drake,' " Pete whispered as the four made their way along the narrow corridor. "You wouldn't be Will Drake, would you?"

The new boy looked surprised. "Yes . . . how did you know?"

Pete stared in turn at Dan and Kate, hoping each would see the connection. Kate cocked her head quizzically. Dan's brow furrowed.

"Yeah, Pete," Dan said slowly. "How *did* you know?"

Pete looked intently at Dan. "Don't you remember? I told you this morning when we met in front of your place. The name in the book—the guy whose clothes I'm wearing—he was forced into the British Navy during the War of 1812! His name was Will Drake! Don't you get it? We're not aboard a reproduction of an old ship. We're on it."

Dan laughed. "Come on," he said with a snort, but his eyes betrayed his weakened confidence. "What you're saying is that we have gone back in time."

"Yeah, Pete," Kate said nervously, her normal self-assurance visibly missing. She had seen for herself Will Drake's name in Pete's book. "You can't be serious." She turned to Will. "What's this all about? Who are you really?"

Will returned Kate's gaze. He was now the one with the mistrusting expression. "I have told you who I am. I must now ask who you are."

Dan shook his head. "I'm not buying this," he said. He turned to his sister. "He's got to be part of some scheme cooked up by Mr. Heuck—and maybe Pete." He turned sharply to Pete. "We saw you talking with Mr. Heuck in the *Bing*. He put you up to this, didn't he?"

Pete shook his head, his grim expression his only response.

"Come on," Dan implored, still staring incredulously at Pete. He faced his sister. "How can we get him to tell the truth?"

"I shouldn't have to tell you anything," Pete interrupted. "Just look around. You said it yourself. There is no ship like this on the Great Lakes—not in our time—not in the 20th century. We have been sailing due east, for what—half an hour now. Have you seen any sign of civilization?"

Kate leveled her eyes at Pete. She then moved to the porthole and gazed across the water. Her face bore a look of alarm. She turned to her brother. "Pete's right," she said anxiously. "We should have passed Prentiss Bay and Beavertail Point. There would have been people, boats and cabins all around. You know something else? It fits with our dreams, too," she said, practically in a whisper.

Dan shook his head. He still wasn't convinced.

"There's one more thing," Pete said, reaching into his jacket pocket. He retrieved the gold-embossed ledger that Dan and Kate had seen earlier. "Remember this?" he said, handing it to Kate.

She held it momentarily before nearly dropping it. "It's hot!" she exclaimed. She passed it hurriedly to her brother. He looked surprised and quickly returned it to Pete.

"Look," Pete said, "I don't think books are supposed to do this, not on their own. What I think is, is that it's not supposed to be here. If it's not, then maybe we're not supposed to be here either. But here we are."

"There's something else, Dan," Kate said. She turned to Pete. "Show him that entry we found this morning." Pete nodded and opened the book so that all four could see. Kate continued, "Look at this— 14 July 1812— W. Drake—that's Will, here. And then there's the next page that has K. and D. Hinken. Remember how we thought they might have been our relatives? Well, I don't think they're our relatives. I think they're us!"

Dan stared grimly at Kate. "Don't be ridiculous," he whispered. "That's impossible."

"There's no other explanation," Kate said. "Look, Dan, I know we've had some weird dreams where we wake up and are able to keep something bad from happening. Maybe this time we have to go into the past to do it. And if Pete's right, we're already there."

Dan stared at each of the three in turn. "If we are in the past, then we're way in the past," he said, shaking his head.

Will Drake watched the three newcomers. "You're all talking rubbish," he said accusingly. "Who are you?"

"Don't ask us how," Pete said, "but it looks like we've come here from another time. An hour ago we were with our friends on our way to a picnic. It was August 29, 1952. Remember the boat we were in, the *Captain Bing*? Did you see any oars or a sail?"

"No," Will said softly, recalling the gray vessel and how it had approached the *Caledonia*. "It was the strangest thing I've ever seen."

"That's because it has a gas engine," Pete added. "You don't have those in 1812, do you?"

Will shook his head. "A gas engine?—What's that?"

"And look at my jacket," Kate said. "Ever see one of these?" She pulled the zipper down and up. "It's a zipper. For you, this won't be invented for another hundred years."

Will had seen enough. He looked into the anxious faces of his fellow conscripts. "And you say you have no idea how you got here?" he asked.

"None," Pete answered.

"More importantly," Kate said, first facing Will and then her brother, "we have no idea how to get back."

"You won't be going anywhere if Skaggs finds out about this," Will said grimly. "He would turn you over to the captain as some sort of enemy to the King. Believe me, they'd make up a reason to toss you overboard. Skaggs is taking us to the ship's store to get you some proper sailors' gear. You'll need to hide those other clothes before people start asking about that 'zip' thing." He turned to Pete. "How come you've got a uniform like mine?"

"It's not *like* yours," Pete answered, measuring his words carefully. "It *is* yours. Back at my cottage, in the

Snows we have a trunk full of old outfits. What I'm wearing has been at the bottom of that chest for over a hundred years. My sister hauled it out for the party we were going to. I had it on when Dan caught sight of this ship." Pete looked into Will's eyes. "Will, I haven't told you who I am. My name is Pete Jenkins, but my mother's name when she was a girl was Drake. Last night, she told me all about you. You are my great-great-great-grandfather."

Will looked intently at Pete for several moments. "Of all the impossible notions, that is the strangest. But from everything I've heard and seen, I have no choice but to believe you." He stared a moment longer. "My own kin," he said, holding his hand out to Pete. "I suppose that means that somehow I live through all of this and have a family. I guess it will be my fatherly duty to keep you safe."

"When you think about it," Pete said seriously, "it's more important that I keep you safe. I don't know where I'd be if anything bad happens to you just now."

Will nodded and then glanced at Dan and Kate. "And who are you? My future cousins?" he guessed.

"No," Kate replied. "I'm Kate Hinken and this is my twin brother Dan. Pete Jenkins is just a good friend."

"Usually, we're the ones who get Pete into jams," Dan said.

"This time it seems the table is turned," Kate added. "And it doesn't look like there's any simple way to turn it back."

CHAPTER 13
LIFE ABOARD THE ENEMY SHIP
JULY 14, 1812

Skaggs led the four Americans up one deck and through a long, dark passageway. Finally, he stopped at a door. The sign above it read "Ship's Store." Skaggs pushed Dan and Kate into the small room and then ordered Will and Pete to follow. "We got some new sailors, Farnsworth," he squeaked.

The large, one-armed man sitting at a wooden desk looked up. Behind him were shelves filled with jackets, shirts, socks, shoes and caps. Drawers were marked "Tobacco," "Pipes," and "Playing Cards."

"Skipper wants these two set up with proper seamen's slops," Skaggs ordered.

Mr. Farnsworth eyed Dan and Kate in their short pants. "Mighty odd-looking duds you two are wearing," he said.

"We're not from around here," Kate said, smiling nervously.

"Yes, well, slops like those won't be much good aboard this 'ere ship," he said. He nodded to Will, having fitted him out that morning. When he saw Pete, already dressed in standard sailor gear, he turned to Skaggs. "Where'd *he* come from?" he asked.

"We picked all three of them off a boat back apiece," Skaggs said. "Caught 'em trying to help their American friend here jump ship," he added, nodding toward Will.

"More Americans, eh?" Farnsworth grumbled. He stood and eyed Dan, sizing him for fit. "This keeps up, ship'll be lousy with spies and traitors." With his one good arm, he gathered a set of clothes, shoes and socks and handed them to Dan. He sat down at his desk, pulled a gilt-edged, leather book from his jacket and inked his quill. Toward the bottom of the right-hand page he wrote the date, 14 July, 1812. "Name?" he asked.

Dan stared at the man's accounts book. He was so distracted that he could barely speak.

"Uh . . . Dan," he finally mumbled.

"And surname?" Farnsworth asked, glancing up at this slow-witted new sailor.

"Oh, yeah, uh, . . . Hinken," Dan said. "H-i-n-k-e-n." He glanced at Pete and Kate as if to say, "Do *you* see what *I* see?"

Farnsworth made the entry, noting the items dispensed and the worth in shillings and pence for each. Kate leaned in to get a closer look.

"You, there," Farnsworth said. "I don't have any clothes for girls. You'll have to do with men's britches, same as everyone else. Name?"

"Kate Hinken," Kate said. She watched as the man entered her name into the ledger exactly as it had appeared in Pete's book. The page read:

14 July, 1812

| D. Hinken | Sailor's slops | 4s 2d | shoes and hose | 1d |
| K. Hinken | Sailor's slops | 4s 2d | shoes and hose | 1d |

As Farnsworth was writing, Will Drake whispered to Pete, "That's the same book you showed us in the bow lockers. How did *he* get it?"

Pete mouthed the answer, "He doesn't have *my* book. I've got *his*."

"I don't suppose either of you have the money to pay for this," Farnsworth said to Dan and Kate. They shook their heads. "Then you'll have to work it off. The captain will tell me when your account is settled."

Since Pete was already dressed for duty, Farnsworth looked him over quickly. He then eyed the young man's bare feet. "You'll need these," he said, reaching into a bin and drawing out two black shoes and a pair of white socks. "I suppose *you* can pay," he added. "I never met a sailor yet who didn't keep a penny aside for a pair of ship's shoes."

Pete remembered what his dad had told him about the penny in his vest pocket. He pulled out the tarnished coin and handed it to Farnsworth. The man inspected it closely, tilted it to the light and glanced curiously at Pete. He then dropped it into a cash box. Again, he opened his ledger to Dan and Kate's entry. The page was full, so he turned the leaf. At the top, he scratched 14 July, 1812. "Name?" he asked.

Pete stared at the man. "Jenkins. . . uh, Pete," he said, stumbling for words. He eyed Kate with a startled look. They had never gone past the page with K. and D. Hinken on it! The man was writing:

14 July, 1812
P. Jenkins   shoes & hose   1d   paid

Pete wanted to pull the ledger from his pocket right then and check the page he hadn't seen but decided against it. Besides, he knew exactly what he'd find.

Mr. Farnsworth then grabbed three rolled-up hammocks and several blankets from a shelf and held them out to the three newcomers. "You'll need these," he said. He inked his pen and added to all three of his latest entries:

101

"All right," Skaggs said, pushing Pete to the door. "Get moving." The four Americans followed the British sergeant back along the corridor, down one level and forward to the bow. They stopped at the padlocked door. It had a one-foot square opening about eye-level so that a guard, standing in the hallway, could see inside. But it also had two vertical iron bars across it to keep any prisoner from escaping.

"I'll have to put all of you in one room," Skaggs snarled. Then he added with a sneer, "It may be tight, but prisoners don't need much space, do they?" He undid the lock and herded the four Americans inside.

"I'm leaving you to change into your new slops," Skaggs said. "Take your time; I'll be back in five minutes." He slammed the door, locked it and left.

Kate was staring at her new pair of shoes. "Will, how do you tell the left from the right?" she asked, turning them around. Dan and Pete each looked at their shoes, as well.

"On a ship like this, it's pretty much 'small, medium and large,'" Will answered.

"All right," Kate said. She set her shoes and socks on the floor and picked up her new clothes. "You guys will have to turn your backs while I get into this outfit."

The boys obliged. By the dim light of the portholes, first Kate and then Dan changed into their uniforms. Pete, meanwhile, put on his socks and shoes. Dan and Kate then hid their modern clothes in a corner under a tattered sail. Shortly, all four Americans were in identical attire, awaiting their next orders from Skaggs.

The British soldier returned and quickly sent Will

Drake to find the captain. Will was to begin his duties as cabin boy, leaving Skaggs to keep the other three busy.

For the rest of the day, the soldier worked Pete, Dan and Kate at odd jobs all over the ship. They were swabbing the quarterdeck near the helm when Moneypenny called out, "Skaggs, get those three over here." He waved them in the direction of an odd-looking device in the middle of the main deck. "Put them on the capstan," he said. "We're raising the topgallant sail!"

Skaggs pushed the three Americans down one flight of stairs to a large, wooden, barrel-shaped wheel. Six heavy spokes stuck out of it about chest high. The three stood looking at it as three sailors dragged a thick hemp line across the deck and secured it to the wheel's hub. The sailors then put their hands on the spokes and looked toward an older bull-of-a-man standing nearby. He held a coiled rope in his right hand. A short brass whistle hung from a chain around his neck.

"Get in here!" he yelled to Pete, Dan and Kate. "Y' think they're going to haul it themselves?" At that, he let the coiled rope fall to the deck, keeping a firm grip on its leather handle. He raised his arm and sent the long rope sliding across the deck behind him. Then, with one arm swing, it flew over the capstan and cracked like a rifle shot. Pete jumped in behind one of the sailors. Dan and Kate also found a pole to hold. None of them had a clue as to what might follow. It looked like the beginning of a Maypole dance, but without the pretty ribbons. All six stood, one behind the other in the circle.

"H'ist her up," Moneypenny ordered.

At that, Pete noticed that the whip-guy took a deep breath. Pete braced himself for a lashing, but instead the man opened his mouth and *sang*. His voice poured out loudly, resonantly and with a measured rhythm, "Our boots and clothes are all in pawn . . ."

Immediately, the other three sailors, leaning into their poles, began to march around the barrel. Pete nearly fell over but caught his balance and stood up. Just then the whip snapped over his head.

Pete quickly got the idea that he was supposed to help push the bar. When the chanteyman finished his line, the other sailors belted out in unison, "Go down, you blood-red roses. Go down."

Then the whip-man sang, "And it's flamin' drafty around Cape Horn . . . "

And the others droned, "Go down, you blood-red roses, go down."

Then all four of the seasoned sailors sang in unison, "Oh, you pinks and posies. Go down, you blood-red roses, go down."

As the wheel turned, the rope filled the capstan barrel. In the topmost part of the *Caledonia*'s central mast, Pete saw a large sail slowly going up.

By the third verse when the chanteyman was singing, "And it's 'round Cape Horn we're off to go . . ." Pete was pushing his pole and singing the chorus like an old salt.

Pete reasoned that the bosun—the guy with the whip—was in charge of keeping the crew in line and seeing to it that the captain's orders were followed. He could do it with pain or pleasure, using a whip or a song, depending on the situation. As the chanteyman, the bosun continued to sing until the topgallant sail was in place.

"Belay!" he yelled, and the sailors stopped. Pete didn't know what "belay" meant, so he continued to push his bar. Without the help of the others, it was like trying to move a house. He realized now how hard the task had been and how important the teamwork of his capstan mates were in raising the sail.

For the rest of the afternoon, the bosun called upon Skaggs to put Dan, Kate and Pete to work.

He had different songs for every task—quick, fast-paced ones for easy jobs and slow, drawn-out ones for harder work. There were capstan chanteys like the first one, and there were halyard chanteys where Pete stood in a long line of men and pulled a rope—sort of like a one-sided tug-of-war set to music. The chanteyman had a seemingly endless number of ditties for any work occasion.

Pete had never heard any of them before. Any songs he ever heard were played on WTAC, the only radio station worth listening to back home. The lyrics were almost always about girls or cars—or very often girls *and* cars. As dumb as they were, they were as good as it got. These chanteyman's songs told of real people, real places, real times in history. Pete suddenly realized these weren't *historical* references for these sailors. They were current events.

In between raising and lowering sails, Skaggs had his three charges barbarize the upper deck, scouring it with a mixture of sand and cleaning powder. After that, they went to the galley to peel potatoes, wash dishes, serve meals and swab the mess area.

By the end of his four-hour shift, Pete was bushed. His back ached. Blisters on his hands and feet raised and promptly broke. His arms and legs felt as if he'd stretched every muscle and twisted it into a knot. He had never worked so hard in his life. Still, in an odd way, he felt a sense of worth at being a useful member aboard this 19th-century ship.

105

CHAPTER 14
WILL DRAKE LEARNS A SECRET

Meanwhile, Will Drake served Mr. Moneypenny his evening meal in the captain's quarters. He mopped the skipper's floor and straightened his wardrobe. And although Moneypenny never said it in so many words, Will knew that being cabin boy was much easier than the tasks he saw his American friends doing. He was sure the captain was trying to make up for Will's having lost his parents.

As Will walked past the captain's desk, he noticed a large book. It was opened to a partially filled page. He read the date: 14 July, 1812. Today! Will thought. This must be the ship's log! He glanced at Moneypenny. The captain had his back to him, studying a chart stretched across a large table. When Will was certain there was no chance of being noticed, he silently turned the ship's log back six pages. There it was: General Brock's orders!

8 July, 1812
Received sealed message from General Isaac Brock. I must take Caledonia to Fort St. Joseph's in the St. Mary's River as soon as possible and report to Captain Charles Roberts of the 10th Royal Veteran Battalion. British military leaders hope American commander at Michilimackinac is unaware of current state of war. I must capture or sink any foreign ship bearing U.S. colours, arrest any deserters and press all able-bodied seamen into service. If requested by Roberts, I am to transfer troops aboard Caledonia to Michilimackinac and

assist in every way I am able. Speed and secrecy are of utmost importance for Britain to recapture the land lost at the Jay Treaty.

Will was reading his parents' death warrant! His hands began to shake. He glanced at the captain to make sure he had not been noticed and quickly returned the book to its original page.

-     -   -   -   -

That evening at eight bells, Skaggs herded his three prisoners to the mess deck. Will was there, waiting for them. Pete saw his troubled expression.

"What's wrong?" Pete whispered.

"I'll tell you later," Will mouthed silently. He nodded to Skaggs who lingered nearby.

Pete heard the bosun's whistle and watched as ten sailors barged past him and went up top. A minute later ten others came down from the main deck, filed into the galley and demanded to be served. The bosun stared at the new recruits while uncoiling his whip, leaving no doubt who the waitstaff would be. At once, the four American prisoners jumped to their feet and served dinner. Pete guessed that half the *Caledonia*'s twenty-member crew would be on duty for a four-hour shift while the other ten would be eating on the mess deck or resting in their fo'c's'le quarters.

Pete was carrying some dirty dishes to the galley when, from above, a high-pitched whistle shrieked. At once, every sailor in the galley bolted up the ladder to the main deck. Pete glanced at Dan and Kate and then followed them up the stairs.

From the west, an ominous black cloud approached. Lightning danced beneath it.

Pete Carries Dishes

"Haul in the canvas!" Moneypenny shouted. "Make haste, men. It's a white squall!"

Every sailor raced about, dropping sails and securing lines. The pleasant sky of only a few minutes before suddenly took on the yellowish tint of a deadly storm. Pete knew firsthand that a white squall could tear a ship this size to pieces in a minute. He joined the others on the center of the main deck. All stood looking anxiously as the menacing thunderhead rolled toward them.

"Captain!" a sailor screamed. "The mains'l's fouled at the topgallant mast!"

"Get someone up there to clear it!" Moneypenny commanded.

The bosun glanced about for available sailors. All were scrambling around, stowing ropes and bolting hatches. His eyes settled on the four Yanks who stood nearby. "Skaggs, get those recruits ready!"

"Step lively," Skagg yelled.

The bosun picked the tallest one. "You there!" he hollered, pointing to Pete. This was the same guy who had cracked the whip over Pete's head while leading the capstan crew with the work songs. "Get up there and clear that line!"

"Me?" Pete said with a gulp. Pete was terrified of heights. He also didn't much care for depths—depths such as he would surely reach if he fell from the heights where the man was pointing. "I don't think I can do that," he mumbled.

"Move!" The bosun shouted, uncoiling his whip. He shoved Pete to the base of the mast. Pete grabbed the rope ladder and put his foot on the first rung. Then he took another step. "Faster!" the man yelled. Pete heard the whip crack above his head. He jumped and took the next several steps two at a time.

Higher and higher he went until he came to a crosstree. The breeze whistled through the rigging, and the *Caledonia* rolled ominously from port to starboard with each whitecap. As the wind blew harder, the ship rocked wilder from side to side. Pete flew back and forth high above the ship's deck, hanging on for dear life as he climbed steadily, if slowly, skyward.

He felt the temperature drop from balmy to frigid in about one minute. As it did, freezing rain began to slap his face. Soon, hail pellets were stinging him like birdshot. His fingers were numb, and his clothes clung icily to his skin. Still, he continued up the mast's rigging.

At last, he reached the fouled rope. He tugged at a line, and the canvas sail dropped.

As it did, Pete lost his balance. For a moment, he was airborne. He dropped like a rock from the topgallant mast a hundred feet in the air. In a split-second he glimpsed his death—either smashing on *Caledonia*'s deck or dropping like an anchor to the floor of Lake Huron. Then, with a sudden snap, his left ankle became snagged in the sail's rigging.

He hung there, dangling like a spider from a tree. He caught sight of Kate below, gasping in terror as she stared up at him. For several moments, he swayed upside down ninety feet in the air. The deck below weaved back and forth beneath him. Pete looked up at his ankle and the rope that held it. With any sudden twist, it would loosen and he would continue his drop to death. He timed a wave and pulled himself slowly to his foot. He grabbed the rope, dislodged the knot, and righted himself, clutching the mainsail with both of his frozen hands.

Slowly, he worked his way to the rope ladder. Once again, he looked down.

Kate, Dan and Will seemed like a mile away. Step by step he descended until, finally, he reached the main deck. He turned around and found himself, once again, staring at the bosun. Instead of a pat on the back and a "Job well done," he got an angry stare and a "What took yeh so long!"

By then, the storm was in full flower. Pete looked past the seaman and saw ropes snapping and sails ripping all over the ship. Sailors were running across the decks, slashing lines with axes and shoving belaying pins into notches.

Then, suddenly, almost as quickly as it had begun, the storm passed. The *Caledonia* rolled less and less with each wave. The decks were a mess, but at least the masts were still pointing skyward.

Skaggs came to the four Americans. "Get below and help in the galley. The sailors are hungry," he squeaked. Pete went down the hatch and the others joined him. For half an hour they served the crew.

When that was done, Kate came to Pete's side and put her arm around his waist. "What you did up there was amazing," she said. "I didn't think you were going to get down alive! How did you do it?"

"I don't know. It all went by kind of fast," Pete said, his cheeks steaming from Kate's embrace. "Besides, I don't remember anyone giving me a choice."

The cook came out of his scullery and saw the four recruits. "Clear those dishes and I'll dole out some grub fer yeh," he said.

Pete stared blankly at the man. He'd forgotten how hungry he was. Breakfast at Mr. Heuck's boathouse had seemed like ages ago, but with all that had happened since, he hadn't had any time to think about food. Now, at the mere mention of it, his mouth began to water.

The chef motioned for the four to come to his kitchen. There, on the floor, stood a wooden bucket filled to the brim with table scraps from the last meal. "It's lobscouse, mostly," the cook said. "Grab a bowl and pick out whatever you like. The rest goes to the seagulls."

Dan and Kate each took a step back, sticking up their noses at the thought of eating other people's garbage.

Pete, however, was not nearly so particular. At least he'd take a look. As he leaned toward the pail, Will moved past him holding a bowl and a spoon, one in each hand. Will hungrily ladled large bits of meat, potatoes, onions and broken hardtack into his wooden dish.

Pete leaned in closer and took a whiff. The meat seemed to have a suspicious odor, but he figured that if Will could eat it, so could he. With Will's bowl full, Pete loaded up his as well. The longer Kate and Dan considered their options—eat garbage or starve—the less picky they became. Before long, all four were sitting at a table, wolfing down their makeshift meal as if it had just been served to them by the owner of the Grand Hotel himself.

Toward the end of their dinner, Kate looked squarely at Dan. "How are we going to get back?" she asked.

Dan knew at once what she meant. He raised his eyebrows and shrugged. "I don't know," he said. "This is new territory. When we've had our dreams before, they've never taken us anywhere like this."

"Dreams," Will said, a spoonful of burgoo poised near his mouth. "You talked about your dreams when we first met. You make it sound as if, in your time, you can make them come true. Can you really do this?"

"No, it's nothing like that," Kate said. "But for Dan and me, some of our dreams are like a warning, usually of something bad. If we can figure them out fast enough, we can keep whatever it is from happening. We don't tell anyone about it because most people would think we were making it up. But we know, and that's all that counts."

Pete leaned in. "Will, I've seen it happen. I know that it works. I think, like their other dreams, we're here to do something. And this time, I had a dream, too. We're here for something important."

Dan looked frustrated. "Like what," he interrupted. "Get ourselves killed in a war that happened 130 years before we were born?"

"This is no dream now," Kate said. "Unless you believe in mass hypnosis."

"I'm not sure what I believe," Will said quietly, "but it seems to me that somehow I'm at the bottom of it."

"What do you mean?" Kate asked.

"The common thread to all of this is my relationship to Pete," Will answered.

"Maybe what Pete said earlier was right. With my parents suddenly gone, he might be here to protect me—to make sure that I survive, and since you two are Pete's friends, you're here to help. I sense that the three of you have had some tight scrapes where you needed each other to get through them. Am I right?"

Dan, Kate and Pete nodded, remembering several times during the summer that one or the other had saved the others' skins. "I suppose that's so," Kate said. "You think those times might have just been getting us ready for this?"

"Just a feeling," Will said with shrug.

"You may be right," Dan said. "Something may be about to happen that the three of us can change because of what we know about the past." He sat back in his chair. "But I have no idea what it is."

Just then Skaggs came down from the main deck to the mess hall. He burst into the galley and shouted at his four prisoners, "The skipper wants you to get some sleep! March!" He pointed to a passageway and led them down one deck to their room. He opened the bows locker and pushed them in. "Sweet dreams," he said as he bolted the door.

The sun broke through the storm clouds and poured light into the small room. The four Americans hung their hammocks, sat down and put their heads together. "Has Captain Moneypenny told you where the *Caledonia* is going?" Dan asked Will.

"That's what I wanted to tell you before the storm," Will said. "I saw it in the ship's log. General Brock is sending the *Caledonia* to some place called St. Joseph's Island. Have you heard of it?"

"Sure," Dan answered. "It's about twenty-five miles east of the Snows in the St. Mary's River. It used to be . . ." then he caught himself. "I mean it *is* the site of a British fort."

"Judging by where the sun set behind us," Kate said, "I'd say that's where we're heading."

"With any wind at all, we'll be there early tomorrow morning," Dan added.

"Why do you think Brock is sending the *Caledonia* there?" Pete asked.

"Who knows?" Dan said. "It's a tiny fort."

Will leaned in closer. "That's the most important part!" he said. "The *Caledonia* is supposed to take the British troops from Fort St. Joseph's to Mackinac Island."

Dan looked thunderstruck. He turned to Will. "What date did you say this is?"

"July 14th," Will said. "Why?"

Dan stared at Kate. "Remember what Mr. Porter said about the British attack in 1812? It happened in the middle of July! I'm sure of it!"

"That's right!" Kate said. "Do you think saving Fort Mackinac is what our dreams were about? Could this be the reason we came back in time—to stop that from happening?"

"Stop what from happening?" Will asked.

"The British attack!" Kate answered.

Dan faced Will and explained. "Kate and I have been coming to Mackinac Island for years," he said. "In our time, it's a great place to ride horses, go biking, walk around—but besides that is all the historical stuff that happened there. And most of that has to do with the British attack in the War of 1812!"

"So you think you're here to stop the British from attacking Fort Mackinac?" Will guessed.

Pete held up his hand, shaking his head. "Look, that doesn't make sense" he said. "Suppose we stop the British from taking the fort. If we do that, then, in reality, it never happened. If it didn't happen, how could we have heard about it in our real time?"

Dan and Kate stared blankly at Pete for a moment. "Yeah, you're right," Dan agreed. "That'd be impossible. Okay, so maybe we don't stop the British from attacking the fort. Maybe we just change how they do it a bit."

Kate stood up from her hammock. "How are we going to change anything?" she asked, raising her hands in exasperation. "Skaggs watches our every move by day and he's got us locked in here at night! We're stuck!"

Pete shook his head. "I don't know," he said, "but if helping Will is the link, then maybe it's our only chance to go back home. We've got to think of something."

"Maybe the answer's in Pete's ledger!" Kate said excitedly. She turned to Pete. "In your book all the pages are filled, right? I wonder if something in there holds the key!"

"Right," Dan said eagerly. "Get it out, Pete. Let's see if we can find a link."

Pete reached into his jacket pocket as the others gathered close by. He pulled out the ledger and thumbed through its pages. He quickly found the entry for when they got their clothes. He then turned to the next page and saw, for the first time, his own entry. Then there were several accounts of sailors with names like Thompson, Johnson, and Baylor, who bought small articles such as tobacco and playing cards. None seemed terribly important. On the next page was written:

16 July, 1812 10 p.m.
off Goose Island, Straits of Mackinac
M. Dousman   hammock and bedding   loaned

"M. Dousman," Kate said with a shrug. "Never heard of him either."

"I have!" Dan exclaimed eagerly. "He's the guy Mr. Porter told us about at the fort. I don't remember exactly what he did, but I know that's the name."

Will glanced from face to face, hoping that one of them would remember the missing piece of the puzzle and spit out the entire story.

None of them did. After a long silence, Pete muttered, "Do you know how weird this is? According to my book, this M. Dousman won't come aboard until the day after tomorrow! It's not strange enough that we go back in time to do something, which we don't know what it is, but now we're reading about what will happen from something that was written before it happens! Does that make sense to anyone?"

"Not much does anymore," Dan said.

Kate shook her head. "It's weird, all right." She

looked over Pete's shoulder.

"What's the next entry? Maybe there's a clue there."

Pete scanned the next several pages, scouring each item carefully. "There's nothing but guys buying tobacco and cards and stuff," he said. "This one for Dousman is our best bet—at least he's someone we've heard of."

"Think hard, Dan," Kate said. "You're the history whiz. What does this Dousman guy do?"

Dan closed his eyes. After several moments he shook his head. "It's no use. I can't remember," he said. "It's one of those things—you know the answer, but the harder you try, the harder it is to think. Maybe later it'll just pop into my head. Whatever it is, I know it must be important—and it must be why we're here."

All four finally leaned back in their hammocks, pulled their blankets over themselves and soon were fast asleep.

The *Caledonia* plowed ahead on its easterly course from the Les Cheneaux Islands toward the St. Mary's River. A steady wind held during the night and brought the *Caledonia* to the mouth of De Tour Passage.

Inside their locked bows quarters, four young American sailors slept soundly. Gradually, the gray dawn disclosed the tall ship creeping up the St. Mary's River to the southern tip of St. Joseph's Island. The timbered walls of the small British fort came into view.

CHAPTER 15
THE MESSAGE ARRIVES AT ST. JOSEPH'S ISLAND
15 JULY, 1812 5 a.m.

The sun hadn't yet risen when a sweet, cedar scent swept through the *Caledonia*'s portholes and into the cramped quarters of the four American prisoners. Outside, a seagull's scream split the air, shattering the silence. For Pete Jenkins, it was not an unfamiliar sound. He had been awakened often in his cottage by such a wild racket. Now, he rolled in his hammock, groggily trying to remember the dream he was having. It was so real. Kate was in it. So was Dan. They were aboard an old-fashioned pirate ship, sailing to some historic fort.

Pete slowly became aware of how unusual his bed felt. For one thing, it was moving—rolling from side to side. For another, it sounded as if water was splashing on his bedroom walls.

He opened his eyes, and in the faint light he saw three gray hammocks swinging lazily from the ceiling. People were in them. This was not a dream, nor was this rope hammock his cottage bed. Reality swept over him like a cold flood.

From above, Pete heard the call, "Drop anchor!" It was Mr. Moneypenny. A splash followed just outside. Pete glanced at his roommates. All were still asleep. He rolled from his hammock and moved to a porthole. He pressed his face to the opening and looked down. Inches below, water swirled along the *Caledonia*'s hull. We must be on a river, he reasoned. He gazed forward past the bowsprit and noticed that the *Caledonia* was barely twenty yards from land.

A Seagull's Scream Split The Air

He could see, lining the shore, dozens of birchbark canoes. Scattered among them were several boats resembling the *Captain Bing*, but without inboard, gas-powered engines. Just beyond the beach stood an entire village of crude shacks, teepees and wigwams. Farther up the hill was a small fort, encircled by a wall of spike-tipped logs. Here and there, human shapes moved through the setting like ghosts in a mist.

Suddenly, Pete was startled by the wrenching sounds of a nearby pulley. He turned and looked back along the port side of the *Caledonia*. A davit was lowering a narrow boat into the river. Facing forward in its bow was Mr. Moneypenny. In the stern was Sergeant Skaggs, dressed in his best military uniform. Between them were three *Caledonia* seamen, each holding a pair of oars. When the boat settled into the water, Moneypenny and Skaggs released the davit hooks, and the three sailors began to row upstream.

Pete looked again toward shore. Through the clinging haze he saw a man standing at the end of a short dock. His military uniform was clearly that of a British Army officer.

Pete turned to Dan's hammock and tugged his arm. "Dan!" he said, "I think we're at Fort St. Joseph's. The captain and Skaggs are taking a boat to shore."

Dan lifted his head, rubbed his eyes and set his feet down from his rolling bed. He hurried to the porthole and whispered, "Duck! They're coming alongside. We can't let them know we're watching."

Pete dropped to the floor. Dan quickly crawled to the other two hammocks. He nudged Kate and Will. "Wake up!" he whispered. Both rolled out immediately.

The small boat passed so near that any one of the prisoners could have reached out through a porthole and grabbed an oar, but all four stayed out of sight.

In moments they were back on their feet and huddled around the two portholes. Will and Pete took turns peeking through one, while Dan and Kate shared the other. The oarsmen were straining to make headway against the strong current. At times, they actually lost ground as the swirling waters pushed them downstream toward the *Caledonia*.

About halfway to the dock, Moneypenny cupped his hands to his mouth. "Ahoy! Captain Roberts! Good to see you," he called.

"Ahoy yourself, Moneypenny," Roberts blustered. "What's the news?"

"You know about the war?" Moneypenny asked.

"Yes, yes, yes," Roberts replied heatedly. "I've known about that for a week. Come now, Moneypenny, get on with it."

"Perhaps our message should not be overheard," Moneypenny replied cautiously, glancing suspiciously along the shoreline.

"We are among friends," Captain Roberts exclaimed in exasperation. "You know, you really should have brought abler men to escort you. By the time you get here, the war may be over."

Moneypenny smiled sheepishly as his oarsmen struggled to make progress. "General Brock has sent a messenger," Moneypenny said. "This is Sergeant Skaggs. Skaggs, meet Captain Roberts, commander of Fort St. Joseph's."

Skaggs jumped to his feet and raised his right hand to salute the captain. As he did, the narrow craft tipped dangerously to one side. Skaggs dropped to his seat, his face flushed with embarrassment.

From behind the portholes, the four Americans could barely stifle a laugh.

"Come, come, soldier!" Captain Roberts demanded.

"Get on with it."

Skaggs gathered himself to speak, still holding his salute. "General Brock's orders are to attack Fort Michilimackinac."

"Huzzah to that," Captain Roberts said with a note of sarcasm.

Skaggs continued. "He wants you to strike before the American commander learns that a state of war exists."

Charles Roberts' expression changed from annoyance to surprise. "Can that be true?" he said. "If I've known of the war for over a week, surely Lieutenant Hanks at Fort Michilimackinac must know of it as well."

"I have reason to believe he does not," Moneypenny replied. "Two days ago, we sank a large American passenger ship just south of the Straits. Only one young man survived. I questioned him and he was not aware that war was on. Yesterday, we plucked three more Americans out of the strangest little boat I ever did see. They also had no knowledge of the hostilities—or anything else, for that matter," he added with a laugh.

Dan pulled his head back from the porthole and whispered to the others, "He'd be surprised at what we know."

Finally, the *Caledonia*'s oarsmen drew the rowboat up to the dock.

"Come ashore, gentlemen," Captain Roberts said.

Skaggs, in his haste to greet the officer, stepped on the gunnel of the slender boat. It tilted dangerously, and once again he lost his balance. Roberts grabbed him by the coat and hauled him up to the dock.

"I'm sorry, sir. Thank you, sir," Skaggs said, scrambling to his feet. His face now matched his crimson jacket for color.

Captain Roberts turned to Moneypenny. "Haven't you taught this soldier anything about boats?" he said with

Captain Roberts

a laugh.

"It's been a busy sail," Moneypenny said dryly.
"Anyway, Brock asked that the *Caledonia* escort your
troops to Michilimackinac. How soon can you be ready?"

"Tomorrow morning," Captain Roberts replied. "John
Askin and Bob Dickson are already here. Each has
enlisted many French-Canadian fur traders and hundreds
of Indian warriors. Actually, the men have been
gathered here for over a week, but I must have a day to
load the provisions. I believe, from what you've said,
that we will make short work of Fort Michilimackinac."

"How can you be so sure?" Moneypenny asked.

"If what you say is true," Roberts said, "and our
attack is unexpected, my plan is to land by night and
approach the fort from the back of the island. We will
bring a cannon and our troops to the heights behind
the fort. When morning comes, we will storm the north
sally port and wipe them out in an hour's time. With
Michilimackinac in our hands, Britain will control the
entire upper lakes, cutting off all American supply
routes to their western forts. They'll fall like dominoes.
Soon, the Yanks will give back to Britain what
Parliament should never have ceded. By next year, we
will control the entire continent."

Back at the *Caledonia*, Pete turned to Dan. "Did you
hear that?" he said. "The English think they can take
back the entire country!"

"And it sounds as if they can do it," Dan replied.

"Look," Kate said. "Captain Roberts is calling some
men to him from the fort."

As she spoke, two men walked down the shore to the
dock. "Mr. Askin, Mr. Dickson, come! I have good
news," Captain Roberts said. "We will hoist anchor for
Michilimackinac tomorrow morning."

Captain Roberts then faced Sergeant Skaggs. "I believe you have delivered your message," he said. Then, to Moneypenny he added, "You may return to your ship, sir. Prepare your men to take aboard my entire garrison and such food, guns and supplies as we will need." He then turned to the two British fur traders and walked with them to shore.

Skaggs saluted and stepped carefully from the dock onto the longboat's stern thwart. Moneypenny lowered himself into the bow and they were off. The rowboat turned and moved swiftly downstream to the *Caledonia*.

Pete and his friends pulled back from their portholes as the oarsmen glided by. Soon, Pete heard pulleys screeching and saw the rowboat being hoisted to the *Caledonia*'s deck.

"They're going to wipe out Fort Mackinac," Dan said grimly. "I don't remember exactly, but I don't think that's how it's supposed to happen."

"Then maybe this is why we're here," Kate said.

"I have no idea how we can change anything," Dan said, "or what it would be if we could."

As they spoke, Pete heard footsteps along the hallway. A key clanked in the lock, and Skaggs pushed the door open. He saw his charges moving quickly away from the portholes.

"What have we here?" Skaggs called out. "You've been spying, haven't you?"

"Yeah," Dan said, a smile creeping across his face. "And we saw you nearly take a header into the drink."

Skaggs scowled and his face began to darken. "I'll send you ashore and put you in stocks," he squeaked. "When I tell the Indians there that you are Americans, they'll take some sass out of you. You won't think yourselves so clever then!"

CHAPTER 16
A DAY ON ST. JOSEPH'S ISLAND

"Up on deck with all of you," Skaggs ordered, shoving the four Americans out of their bows locker. He turned to Will. "The captain will be wanting you to serve him his breakfast. The rest of you will work in the galley."

For the next hour, Pete, Dan and Kate cleaned dishes and swabbed the galley floor. Those tasks done, they ate once again from the sailors' leftovers. They had just finished putting dishes away when Skaggs entered the mess deck. Will Drake followed close behind.

"You're all going to the fort," Skaggs said. "Captain Roberts needs help, and Moneypenny is sending you. You'd better hope the Indians don't find out you're Yanks."

Five minutes later, with Skaggs watching from the main deck, the Americans boarded a small boat and rowed to shore. They beached it and made the short hike to the fort. There, a British soldier, a thin old man in a ragged uniform, motioned them to pass through the gate. "Captain Roberts is expecting you. He's at his quarters," the sentry murmured, pointing to a small, whitewashed house a few yards away. Pete saw an open door and a man stepping through it. It was the officer he had seen on the dock earlier that morning.

"There you are," Captain Roberts said pleasantly. He stood before Dan and Kate. "Moneypenny tells me you two are twins. I have someone here I'd like you to meet."

At that, a huge man appeared from inside the house, completely filling its doorway. He ducked his orange-red mane as he stepped onto the porch. Clenched between his teeth was a clay pipe, which he puffed, sending large clouds of gray smoke over his head. A full beard and heavy moustache surrounded the pipe, masking his facial expression, but his eyes danced under bushy eyebrows and flashed an air of cheer and friendship. He was wearing a plaid flannel shirt under a tan deerskin jacket. Heavy woolen pants, knee-high buffalo-skin boots and a red sash completed the woodsman's outfit.

"Och, now, you must be the Americans Mr. Moneypenny was telling us about," he said with a booming Scottish accent. "I'm Robert Dickson, but my Sioux family calls me Mascotapah. It means red-haired man—can't imagine where they got that, eh?" He chuckled amiably as he strode across the small porch. Before he got to the step, two smaller versions of himself appeared at the doorway.

Though slighter of build and darker skinned, both had reddish hair and bore unmistakable kinship to Mascotapah. "These are my children. Twins they are, and about the age of you two, I should guess," he said, as he gazed at the blond-haired Dan and Kate. "Fourteen years have we spent in the west with my wife, To-to-win, the sister of Chief Red Thunder. This summer, they have come with me to learn more of white man's ways."

The two stood silently behind their father, staring at the American visitors. Mr. Dickson motioned his children to his side.

"This is my son, Ojeeg, and my daughter, Leelinau," he said. "They will be going into the woods soon to

Robert Dickson

collect materials to make war paint. Much will be needed for the hundreds of warriors who will be going tomorrow to Fort Michilimackinac. I hope you are willing to help them."

Kate stared the huge Scot in the eye. "You want *us* to help *you* with your attack on *our* fort?" she asked incredulously.

Pete clearly saw a smile break from behind Mr. Dickson's thick beard.

"I thought you might enjoy some time away from scrubbing decks," the Scotsman said. "It's a beautiful day to be in the woods—but then they all are, as far as I'm concerned." He turned to his children, "You won't bite the nice Americans, will you?"

The two broke their stoic expressions and laughed heartily. The boy stepped toward Kate. "My sister and I would like to know more about your people," he said. He spoke perfect English, though with a bit of a Scottish accent.

His sister came to his side. She was only slightly shorter than Ojeeg and had an engagingly beautiful face. Her clothes, although resembling those of her brother, were fashioned of soft deerskin with much beadwork sewn in. "My mother's people have told us only the bad things about American people," Leelinau said in a liltingly sweet voice. "But my father says there are always two sides to every story. He has brought us here to learn for ourselves and form our own opinions."

Mr. Dickson removed the pipe from his mouth and looked earnestly into the faces of the four Americans. "How about doing this as a favor to me?" he said. "If you are *very* convincing of your ways, you may even gain two converts to your side."

Kate glanced at Dan, Pete and Will in turn. Each

130

nodded assent, Dan perhaps more eagerly than the others. He couldn't take his eyes from Mascotapah's daughter. Leelinau blushed and turned to her father.

Kate spoke up. "We won't have to wear any war paint ourselves, will we? When our soldiers cream your guys, I don't want any of them to think we were on your side." She said it boldly but knew full well the British would capture the fort by noon the next day.

At that, Mr. Dickson laughed. "No. No war paint for the Americans."

Kate smiled. "Then we'll go." She turned to Leelinau. "What would you like us to do?"

"Come, we have many baskets you can help us carry," Leelinau answered. At that, she turned to her father. "We will be back soon." She motioned for the others to follow. Soon the little group had moved past the fort's gate and into the village of small huts and Indian tents. Ojeeg entered a tall teepee and came out a moment later carrying six reed baskets.

He handed one to each of the others and then said, "Follow me; we have much to do. We will begin with small things—berries and roots from the high ground. They are harder to find but lighter to carry. Then we will gather the heavy clay from the river."

CHAPTER 17
WAR PAINTS AND BATTLE PLANS

The six walked back through the crude village and around the fort's picket walls. Ojeeg led them along a trail that would take them through a clearing and into the nearby forest. Before entering the woods, Leelinau stepped in front of her brother and faced the four Americans. She smiled and said, "Father has told you that I am Leelinau and my brother is Ojeeg. If we are to go into the forest together, we must know your names in case of danger."

"Of course, you are right," Kate replied. "I am Kate Hinken and this is my brother Dan. These are our friends, Pete Jenkins and Will Drake."

Leelinau and Ojeeg glanced at each other. "Your names sound funny to us," Ojeeg said. "What do they mean?"

"Mean?" Kate answered, looking puzzled. "Our names have no special meaning."

"Your names have no meaning?" Leelinau asked. "How can that be?"

"Our parents give a first and a middle name," Kate said. "They're usually for someone they want us to be like when we grow up. And then we have a last or family name. What do your names mean?"

"My father called me Leelinau because my birthplace is the island which, in my native language, is called Mishen Imokinakog or Place of the Great Turtle-Spirits. You may know it as Michilimackinac. It is sacred to many of our people. Mishen Imokinakog has many beautiful and romantic places. My father, when he came here, met our mother there. They fell in love and married. He named me Leelinau for the spirit who dwells in the *manitowak*, the sacred place where Ojeeg and I were born."

Pete, having been all over Mackinac Island the past two weeks, could picture many such places where this manitowak might be—Ann's Tablet by the fort, Dwightwood Spring on the eastern shore, Croghan Water near British Landing.

Ojeeg then stepped forward. "My name means the fisherman," he said. "Ojeeg is the *manito* or spirit who always returns to his tribe with venison or a full catch of fish from the woods and waters. Ojeeg is revered by our people because he shares all that he brings with the rest of the tribe. Where his spirit dwells, the tribe never wants for food."

"I like your way better," Kate said. "I wish I could be named for something I did rather than for someone I never knew."

Ojeeg then moved closer to Pete and Will. He gazed carefully at each, noting their faces, sizes and builds. "Are you not brothers?" he finally asked.

"No, not brothers," Pete said, taken aback by Ojeeg's question. It was almost as if he knew their secret. "But we are related—distantly."

Pete saw Leelinau look quickly at her brother. He could tell that a message had passed between them, but he could not guess what it might be.

After a few moments, Leelinau said, "I must tell you that my brother and I sometimes have dreams so real they're like signs of something about to happen. When they are particularly clear, we tell them to each other the next morning. We have found that they often come true."

As Leelinau said this, Kate glanced at Dan. These twins had the same extraordinary ability that they had! Pete noticed Dan and Kate's expressions and knew they were remembering their dreams of two nights before—the ones about the tall ship.

"This morning," Leelinau continued, "Ojeeg came to me at first light and told me that in his dream he had met a boy and girl—twins like ourselves—and two others who were as alike as brothers—but were not. I, too, had such a dream. In it, four white people came on a tall ship from a faraway place—perhaps from another time. They came here to bring harmony to both of our peoples."

"When we looked out on the river and saw your ship," Ojeeg said, "we hoped the vision would be more than a dream. We asked our father to speak with the ship's captain to find out if such people might be aboard. He learned that four Americans, two twins and two others, had been captured and were serving on the ship. When he told us that, we asked if we could meet them. He said he would arrange it. Now that we have met you, we believe our dream will come true, and peace will come of it. Is it true that you have come from another time?"

Dan and Kate looked at each other, surprised by the straightforward way the tribal twins had asked such a strange question. "What would make you think that?" Dan asked. An expression of concern over revealing their secret was evident in his eyes.

"It was so in our dreams," Leelinau said candidly.

Finally, Kate answered. "Three of us have," she said, nodding to her brother and Pete. "But we have told only Will about it. We have been afraid of what the British would do to us if they found out. It is not

135

something that many people would believe."

"Moving through time and traveling great distances is not so mysterious to us," Ojeeg said simply. "Gitchee-manito, the Great Spirit, is able to do many such wonderful things for his children. There are countless legends of our brothers and sisters journeying from place to place and from time to time to help others. When their tasks are complete, they swiftly return to their tribes."

"Maybe so," Dan said, "but if it's all the same with you, we'd sort of like to keep it a secret from the British. They may not be as understanding."

"So, you do not know why you're here?" Ojeeg asked.

"We're not sure," Dan said, "but it might be to protect Will from some danger. You see, he is Pete's forefather from many generations in our past. His parents were killed only a few days ago by the British."

"We will keep your secret, if that is your wish," Ojeeg said. He nodded to his sister, and Leelinau lifted her basket and moved toward the forest. The morning sun poured down upon the grassy meadow. The pleasant coolness of the northern Michigan morning would soon give way to the stifling heat of the July day. "Come with me," Leelinau said, stepping barefooted onto a narrow path. Will and Kate followed single file behind her. Then came Ojeeg, Dan, and finally Pete. Pete felt a cool darkness close in around him as the dense canopy of verdant trees swallowed up the sky.

Soon, the six new friends moved up a gradual slope. Pete noticed that the ground was becoming harder beneath his feet and the path somewhat wider.

"We will start here," Leelinau said. She stepped off the path and, bending near a towering oak, gathered handfuls of partially decayed leaves from the forest floor. "These we will use to make a reddish-brown hue," she said. Dan and Kate helped fill her basket.

"Pete and Will, please come with me," Ojeeg said. The two boys moved to Ojeeg's side, where there was a thick growth of bushes. Bright red berries filled the branches. "We will load your basket with currants," Ojeeg said to Pete. "Over there are the blue holly berries. We will fill Will's basket with them."

For the next hour, the six gathered various berries and leaves. Next, they moved from the island's high ground to a trail where the footing was softer and the air cooler.

Farther along, Pete began to hear rushing water. Soon they were at the edge of the St. Mary's River, far upstream from the *Caledonia*. Leelinau stepped from the bank into the current. She made her way to a small cove where thick, green moss grew along its edge. She took some of it and set it on a flat rock to dry.

Meanwhile, Ojeeg dug into the river bottom and lifted handfuls of heavy clay and put it into his basket. As he moved along the bank, he stopped suddenly. Something had caught his eye. He lifted the frond of a tall fern, reached down, and carefully deposited a pile of blue duck dung into a small leather pouch. "This will make Chief Red Thunder happy," he said with satisfaction. "It is his favorite color."

"We must return to camp to prepare the paints," Leelinau said as she added the drained moss to her basket. She stepped from the river onto the bank. "There is much work to be done."

CHAPTER 18
LUNCH WITH THE ENEMY

All six hoisted the baskets onto their backs, placed the wide handles over their foreheads, and followed Leelinau along a narrow trail back toward the fort.

"By the time we return to camp, the afternoon meal should be ready," Ojeeg said. "I hope you will share it with us."

At the mention of lunch, Pete remembered the duck droppings in Ojeeg's pouch. His stomach turned, and he tried to think of a way out of the offer. He then remembered what he had been eating aboard the *Caledonia* and changed his mind. He nodded to Dan, who seemed eager to accept the invitation.

"That sounds great," Dan said. "We have never eaten Indian food."

"It is not just our native fare we will be having," Leelinau said. "There are many French and British men here as well. Each adds his dishes to the others. At a camp such as this, everyone shares what he has. Ojeeg and I are used to being with them for such gatherings. Meals are always a mixture of many different cultures."

"Much as my sister and I are a blend of peoples," Ojeeg said. "You have met our father, Mascotapah. He was born in Scotland and came to Michilimackinac to become a fur trader. Our mother is To-to-win, sister of our chief, Masko An-imi-ki-ka, known by white people as Red Thunder. So, my sister and I are both Sioux, like our mother, and white like our father."

"Your father is a famous explorer and your mother is Indian royalty," Kate said excitedly. "That must make you a favorite of both peoples."

"Yes, sometimes," Leelinau said hesitantly.

"Or neither," Ojeeg added. "Sometimes it is more a curse than a blessing. Often our full-blooded Sioux friends see our red hair and lighter skin and exclude us from tribal affairs."

"And when white people see our features and tribal clothes, they treat us as if we were savages," Leelinau added.

"We can speak the languages native to both our mother and our father," Ojeeg continued, "but we are often kept from the affairs of either race. My father has seen our frustration and says that we must learn to seek its advantages. He says there are two sides to every story."

"We have tried to understand what good can come from being considered outsiders by so many," Leelinau said. "And yet we know it can be done. We have watched our father persuade people of many nations to do what he suggests. He has convinced Sioux, Winnebago and Menominee tribes to come here from great distances to help their British brothers."

"That's the part I don't get," Pete said. "Why are so many Indians willing to help the British? I didn't think Indians trusted *any* white men."

"That is part of the problem," Ojeeg said. "My father says that, over the years, Indians have trusted too many people. It began long ago. First came the *chi-moko-mon*, the French explorers. They were looking for a route to the Orient to trade for spices. They didn't find it, but they *did* find a land filled with beaver, buffalo, fox and deer, which they could kill and skin to make warm clothes. Soon they realized that pelts from these animals were worth more than all the spices in China.

The Frenchmen traded white man's goods—blankets, knives and guns—to our people for pelts. As business partners, the French and the Indian became friends. Soon, many of the French traders married Indian women and had children. They were no longer simply business partners—they were family."

"Then the British came. They didn't like the French and showed little respect for the Indian," Leelinau said. "The British and French fought and, of course, most of the Indian nations sided with the French. But the British won, so most of the French left. Then it was the British who needed the Indians to trap the animals. Soon, they began to get along. Not long after that, way to the east, the British people who had settled in the colonies started their own government, breaking away from the King. Again there was a war, and in that one most of the Indian nations sided with the British. The new country, the United States of America, won the war, and their leaders started pushing the Indians off the land. Farther and farther west they moved, greedy for the hunting grounds the Indian had used since the dawn of time."

Ojeeg added, "Still, some British stayed here to carry on the fur trade. They told the Indian chiefs that if they would help them against their new enemy, the Americans, they could stop them from settling on the Indian hunting grounds. That brings us up to now. Another war between the new country and England has started. That's why we are here—to help the British stop the Americans from taking over any more land. Maybe we can get back what we have lost."

Pete stepped forward. "In our time we have been told that all the Americans wanted to do was to improve the country by settling it and making it more civilized," he said. "Our schools teach us that the Indians were stubborn and unreasonable to stop Americans from making farms and starting towns on the frontier."

Kate turned to Leelinau. "I guess, as your father says, there *are* two sides to every story," she said.

The six moved along the riverbank into the center of the village. Many Indian women were preparing the noonday meal for the camp. One rang an iron triangle to signal that it was ready. Soon, several Indian and Canadian men gathered around.

Ojeeg raised his arms to the crowd. He turned to the people who now encircled his four new friends. In the Sioux language he announced, "Please welcome these Americans who have come with the British ship from a great distance. Without them, we could not have gathered all the materials to make the war paint." As he said this, Leelinau stood near her new friends and whispered Ojeeg's words in English.

Pete looked around as the tribesmen grumbled to each other. He moved closer to Leelinau. "Did he have to tell them that we were Americans?" he whispered.

"They would have found out soon enough," Leelinau answered. "It's better coming from us now."

Ojeeg continued, "Our friends have worked very hard, and we have invited them to share our meal. Please, welcome them as our guests."

Several Indian women standing nearby nodded to the four Americans, their stoic expressions showing little sign of acceptance. They quickly returned to their iron pots, suspended over the fires by tall, wooden tripods. Steam rose from each kettle and with it wafted a variety of strong aromas.

Pete was feeling very uncomfortable amid the hostile crowd. To escape the Indians' penetrating stares, he

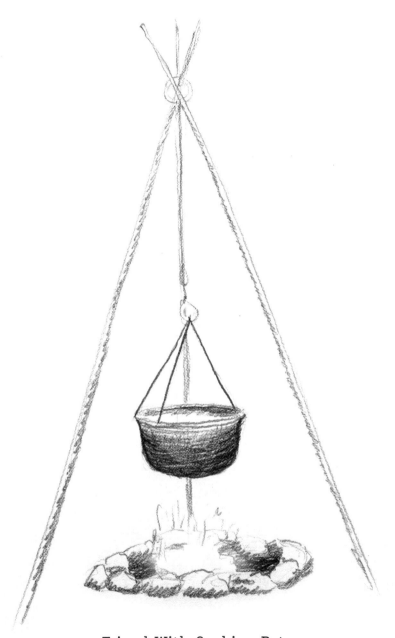

Tripod With Cooking Pot

stepped to the nearest fire and peered into the pot. "This smells okay," he said to a nearby woman.

"It is *zush-ka-boo-bish*—you call muskrat. We skin and cut up," she said in broken English while signing with her hands in a cutting motion. "We add to pot with *pin-ik* and *nee-mush*."

"Uh-huh," Pete said, his enthusiasm waning. Pin-ik and nee-mush, whatever they were, didn't sound like anything he cared to add to his diet, and muskrat was definitely out of the question.

He poked his nose into the next pot. "What's this?" he asked hopefully.

"Na-bo-be—fish soup," the woman said. Pete's eyes brightened. He had never met a fish he couldn't eat. The woman took the stirring ladle and brought a large chunk to the surface. Pete found himself staring into the enormous mouth of the ugliest fish he'd ever seen. Its jaws were open as if to strike—and Pete was its next meal. Broth with bits of onions and kernels of corn dripped from the beast's jaws.

Pete was so surprised that he jumped quickly away. As he did, his left heel snagged Kate's basket of berries, and he stumbled backwards. He landed on the ground with his head in the lap of an old Indian woman who was sitting cross-legged behind him. She stared down into Pete's eyes. Her wrinkled face stretched into a huge smile. A howl of laughter arose from all around. Immediately, the icy tension was broken.

Pete jumped to his feet, glancing sheepishly at the grinning faces surrounding him. He smiled and looked again at the kettle, this time from several feet away. "So, what kind of fish *is* that?" he asked.

"Sturgeon," the woman said with a giggle. "Do not

worry. We do not eat head."

"Oh, okay," Pete said, looking relieved.

"Only eyes," she added. "Help you see far."

Pete again felt ill.

"Wiissini," the woman continued, motioning with her hands to her mouth. "Eat. You like." She pushed her ladle deep into the pot and brought up a portion with large chunks of fish, corn, onions and something that looked like milkweed pods. She poured it into an earthen bowl and handed it to Pete. "Is good," she said, still grinning.

Before long, Pete and the others were sitting cross-legged on the ground in the midst of as diverse a crowd as he had ever seen. The lady was right. The chowder was great. He even tried some of the zush-ka-boo-bish, which he thought sounded better than muskrat. Although it might not have been his first choice at a restaurant, it was certainly a lot better than what he'd been getting aboard the *Caledonia*.

When the meal was over, Ojeeg came and stood before the four Americans. "We would like you to meet our uncle, Chief Red Thunder. He and my father are coming now to help the other men make war paint. They will be pleased to see what we have collected."

Pete followed Ojeeg's gaze and saw two men rowing upstream from the *Caledonia*. He knew that the large man with the flaming red hair was Mascotapah. The other must be their new friends' uncle. The two men beached their boat and came straight to the gathering place.

"This is Red Thunder," Ojeeg said, getting to his feet. The four Americans also stood to meet the Sioux chief. "Uncle, these are our friends—Dan and Kate Hinken, who are twins like us, and Pete Jenkins and Will Drake.

145

They have traveled a great distance to be with us. We have spent the morning gathering materials for war paint."

Chief Red Thunder nodded, his stony expression showing no emotion.

"I bear orders from Skaggs," Mr. Dickson said. "Your friends must return to their ship." He turned to the four Americans. "I think the sergeant misses you," he added with a wry smile. He nodded toward the *Caledonia*. "You may use the boat Red Thunder and I just brought to shore." Pete glanced up at the tall ship. There, standing at the railing and staring down at them, was Sergeant Skaggs, his sour expression having changed little since that morning.

"We will see you tomorrow," Ojeeg said, gazing intently into the eyes of each of his new friends.

Pete thought about the next day's British attack on the American fort. "It won't be as nice as today," he replied.

At that, each of the boys shook hands while Kate and Leelinau embraced. The four Americans then stepped into the rowboat and, under the watchful eye of Sergeant Skaggs, headed back to the *Caledonia*.

CHAPTER 19
LEAVING ST. JOSEPH'S ISLAND
JULY 16, 1812

It was 5 a.m., two bells on the morning watch. Pete had rolled into his hammock only an hour before. He and the others had finished serving the graveyard shift from midnight to four. As tired as he was, he could not sleep. It could have been the sturgeon chowder or even the zush-ka-boo-bish, but more likely it was knowing that in a few hours he would be part of a huge British fleet bent on taking over his own country. Whatever it was, Pete was wide awake.

He rolled out of his hammock and went to a porthole. A thin rim of light in the east cast an eerie grayness to the morning sky. The chilly St. Mary's River swept icily through the warm air, creating a foggy haze along the island's shore.

"All hands on deck," Captain Moneypenny called to his first mate. Instantly, the shrill piping of the bosun's whistle relayed the message into the sailors' fo'c's'le quarters. Arnold Skaggs awakened with the rest of the crew. He rushed down one deck to his four prisoners.

Dan, Kate and Will were sound asleep. They had fallen into their hammocks without even kicking off their shoes. Pete heard someone coming along the hallway. He guessed it was Skaggs, and the soldier's whiney voice soon proved him right.

"Get moving, you Yankee dogs!" Skaggs screeched, poking his face through the grated cell door.

Dan tumbled to his feet and nudged Will's shoulder. He then shook Kate's arm. Pete, he saw, was already up

147

and standing at the porthole. "What do you want?" Dan muttered to the closed door.

A key was rattling in the lock. "Skipper wants all hands on deck," Skaggs answered. He pushed open the cell door, his lantern leading the way. Kate and the boys shielded their eyes from the flickering light as Skaggs herded them out of their cell to the hallway.

"Get on with you now," Skaggs yapped as he prodded them up the stairs to the main deck.

In the blackish-gray early dawn, the moon and stars cast their glow upon the heavy dew clinging to the ship's rigging. If it weren't for the circumstances, Pete would have thought this was the most beautiful sight he'd ever seen. It reminded him of his mother's antique figurine ship, a fragile, milk-glass vessel with ghostly gray sails and lines spun like gossamer from stem to stern. He had passed it a thousand times in his cottage living room.

"Sergeant!" the captain yelled to the soldier.

"Yes, sir," squeaked Skaggs.

"Get those Americans over to the fort and start loading the ship," Moneypenny ordered. "Captain Roberts will have someone there to tell them what to do."

Skaggs ushered his prisoners down a boarding ladder to a flat-bottomed bateau. He put oars in their hands, and they rowed the twenty yards to the dock. A haggard old redcoat sentry motioned them into the fort. There, men were milling about, carrying supplies to the landing. Robert Dickson stood nearby. At his side were Ojeeg and Leelinau, along with a dozen Sioux and Menominee braves. "Och now, men," the red-haired Scot called to his Indian friends. "We'll be needin' to assist Mr. Skaggs and his fine young Americans wi' the loadin' o' the ship."

Thus began three hours of packing the *Caledonia* with supplies. It took eight of the strongest Canadian men to hoist aboard two of the fort's six-pound field cannon, each weighing over fifteen hundred pounds. It was nearly ten o'clock when Pete looked around and saw dozens of Canadian voyageurs in their colorful attire jumping aboard their bateaux.

Likewise, hundreds of Indian braves streamed out from their wigwams and teepees and sprang into their canoes. Their bodies were painted wildly with the pigments Pete and his friends had helped them make the day before. They shouted riotously as they put paddles into the water and shot their canoes toward the *Caledonia*.

Skaggs motioned for his four prisoners to join one of the Canadian bateaux. "Take us to the ship," Skaggs said to a woodsman. At once, they were escorted to the *Caledonia*. The bateau hove to, and Pete and the others climbed the boarding ladder to the deck.

"Man the sails!" Moneypenny called from his place at the helm. The bosun trilled his whistle, and the crew moved from the main deck up through the crosstrees, setting sails, securing lines and preparing the *Caledonia* for its journey. All twenty of the regular sailors were in place by the time Pete and the others came aboard.

"Man the capstan, Skaggs!" the captain called. "Set the anchor line!"

Skaggs pushed Pete and the others to the capstan wheel. Two sturdy sailors hauled a heavy rope across the deck and attached it to the capstan barrel. They then joined the four Americans and leaned forward against their bars.

"Heave around," the captain ordered.

At once the bosun broke into a chantey. "Was yeh

149

ever in Quebec . . ." he boomed at a measured pace.

In unison, the two veteran sailors and the four rookies responded, "Bonny laddie, hielan' laddie." As they walked around the wheel, they stepped over the anchor cable as it wound slowly onto the barrel.

"I'm not really up for a sing-along," Pete whispered to Will. "You don't suppose we could just push the bar—maybe mouth the words?"

Just then a loud crack snapped above Pete's head. It sounded like a gun had gone off in his ear. The bosun's whip had answered his question. Evidently, singing and pushing *were* of equal importance. Pete looked up and saw the chanteyman glaring menacingly at him. Without breaking a beat, the man continued, "Stowin' timbers on the deck . . . "

Pete sang out with the others, "Bonnie hielan' laddie."

As the bosun was singing his next line, Pete whispered to Will. "Is this anchor *tied* to the ground?"

"We haven't even taken up the slack yet," Will whispered. "We're just pulling the boat upstream. Wait till we get the hook off bottom. Then we'll feel it."

The bosun, still eyeing Pete suspiciously, boomed, "Was yeh ever in Aberdeen . . . "

Endlessly, it seemed, the capstan crew walked around the circle, pushing the spokes. Pete soon realized why the chanteyman had been singing so slowly. He must have known that the six workers could not last long if he hurried them. The whip was an added incentive.

Finally, the skipper yelled, "Belay!" The anchor hung dripping below the bowsprit. "Bitt the cable!" Moneypenny called, and several sailors jumped into place and secured a line to keep the anchor from accidentally running out again.

Pete nearly dropped from exhaustion. As he stretched his back, he saw the awesome sight of twenty men aloft, scurrying around like monkeys in a tropical forest. Pete had once thought that the rigging on Dan's *Griffin* was complicated. It was nothing compared with the *Caledonia*'s miles of ropes and acres of canvas.

The ship turned and moved away from St. Joseph's Island as the bosun rang the ship's bell four times. It was 10 a.m. Pete looked over the side. The *Caledonia* was surrounded by hundreds of canoes and bateaux filled with British soldiers, Canadian woodsmen and Indian warriors. The enormous fleet was sailing to Mackinac Island to attack the United States, and there was nothing Pete or his friends could do about it.

With the sails set and the *Caledonia* underway, there was no immediate task for the four, so Skaggs sent them below to the galley. They settled in a corner and chewed on hardtack, which the cook had handed them for their breakfast. Pete was dog-tired and wanted nothing more than to go back to his bed. Skaggs then led Dan, Kate and Will to the lower deck with Pete dragging himself behind. The four once again fell into their hammocks.

As they did, none of them could have any idea what was happening at the *Caledonia*'s destination.

CALEDONIA
MDCCCIX

Ship's Bell

CHAPTER 20
THAT SAME AFTERNOON
ON MACKINAC ISLAND

A mere forty-five miles to the west, Lieutenant Porter Hanks stood on the rampart above Fort Michilimackinac's south sally port. He leaned over the limestone wall and surveyed the village below.

A soldier approached. "Lieutenant Hanks, sir," Corporal Thomas said, saluting his commanding officer.

"Yes, Corporal, what is it?" Hanks asked.

"I think you should see this," the enlisted man said. He handed the lieutenant his spyglass. "I've just come from town. Down along the shore," he said, pointing to the beach, "the Indians have been behaving very strangely. Instead of bartering with the villagers as they always do, they're avoiding them. Over the past week, many of the tribesmen have left the island in their canoes. And there are hardly any of the regular British traders or Canadian woodsmen to be seen anywhere."

Lieutenant Hanks extended the spyglass and stared for several moments at the few Indians standing by their wigwams along the shore. "Mostly old men, women and children," he said. "Very peculiar, Mr. Thomas. For months we have been expecting word from back east regarding war with England, but no statement has come. I wonder if that message has been intercepted and the Indians know something that we don't. It is quite possible that the tribal chiefs have placed their allegiance with the redcoats. If the war has begun, Captain Roberts at Fort St. Joseph's might be preparing his troops for an attack."

"Maybe you should send some soldiers there," Thomas suggested.

Lieutenant Hanks pondered that notion but then he shook his head. "Too risky," he said as he stared across the Straits' waters. "If war has begun, our scouts would be captured easily. We need a single person—someone who would not be suspected." He faced his junior officer. "Who's here on the Island who might have business at St. Joseph's?"

"Michael Dousman," Corporal Thomas answered quickly. "He has been awaiting a shipment of pelts from his agents in Lake Superior. I've heard him say that they are overdue."

"Summon him at once," Hanks ordered.

With that, the officer saluted and hurriedly left the fort. He saddled his horse and set off for Dousman's farm. Two hours later, the black-bearded Michael Dousman, the Island's foremost citizen, fur trader and farmer, strode through Michilimackinac's north gate. He was large in stature and, as captain of the local militia, high in the standing of the community. Now, the muscular, Pennsylvania-born Dutchman stood before the American commander, his square, bearded jaw set firmly. "What is it?" he asked.

"I need to learn what the British are doing at Fort St. Joseph's," Hanks said. "War between Britain and the U.S. seems imminent."

"And you think it may have begun?" Dousman guessed, realizing the gravity of the meeting.

Hanks placed both hands firmly on the Islander's broad shoulders. He studied the Dutchman's eyes. "How soon can you be ready?"

"I can be in my canoe in two hours," Dousman said.

"It is already late in the day. Will you have trouble crossing to the mainland before dark?" Hanks asked.

Dousman glanced at the sky. "If the weather holds, I'll have no trouble," he said. With that, he saluted the lieutenant, mounted his horse and returned to his farm at the top of the Island.

Late that afternoon, Michael Dousman loaded his canoe and, with Goose Island in sight, he pushed off from Mackinac's northeast shore. He'd have to hurry to reach mainland before nightfall. Straits weather could be fickle. If a storm came up, he would be forced inland to seek shelter. Under perfect conditions, with a clear sky, he could make Fort St. Joseph's by late the next day.

Dousman Makes For Goose Island

CHAPTER 21
A HITCH IN THE PLAN

Dusk was turning quickly to dark as Michael Dousman paddled through the Straits of Mackinac. A slight breeze made for a light chop, but it was nothing this experienced woodsman couldn't control. Still, it did cause him to focus on each stroke as he eyed Goose Island dead ahead. He was about halfway there when, for just a split second, he thought he saw the setting sun reflect against what appeared to be the tip of a ship's mast. He was staring anxiously at the spot when his paddle struck something in the water. There was a tremendous splash as an enormous fish slapped its tail. Michael's paddle flew into the air and landed six feet away. Quickly, the Dutchman reached between his feet and grabbed a reserve paddle.

In the minute it took him to turn his canoe and retrieve the floating oar, darkness along the eastern horizon had become complete. Whatever it was that had caught his eye was now hidden by night. As he thrust his paddle into the black water to continue his journey, he realized he could barely see the nearby mainland. Only the brightening stars provided any visibility at all. He must hurry to stay in sight of the shoreline. If clouds should block the starlit heavens, he would be adrift in a sea of black. He knew that using the direction of the waves as a guide was dangerous business, for if the wind shifted, dead reckoning could be a fatal alternative. Lake Huron was no place to be on a dark night.

Starlight held as he stroked toward his target. The

whoosh of the paddle and the warm, southwesterly breeze gave Michael comfort as he proceeded toward Goose Island.

Slowly, from directly ahead, he began to hear the sound of geese—or maybe a flock of ducks. No, it was voices . . . human voices! Someone is approaching, Michael thought. And they must be very near. He stopped and listened but could not tell if they were English, French or Indian, for he thought he heard snatches of each tongue. He could tell only that there were many of them. It was possible that they were his friends, perhaps even his own voyageurs returning to Michilimackinac, but he could not take any chances. He had to avoid them.

Dousman saw the moon's rim just beginning to peek over the eastern horizon. Its ascent would soon brighten the entire sky, and in minutes the Straits would be flooded in silvery light. He turned his canoe sharply to the left. He had taken only three or four pulls, when, realizing that the voices were now coming from all around him, he withdrew his paddle from the water and stopped. He hoped that, by remaining perfectly still, he might go unnoticed. He scarcely breathed as he watched vague silhouettes of an immense fleet of small boats and canoes sweep by.

Suddenly, from just a few feet away, he heard a shout. "Une bateau!" a Frenchman called.

"Can this be true?" another responded, questioning the first. This voice was practically beside Dousman.

"Yes, I see it too!" another voice rang out in French.

Several boats joined the others, coming to Dousman's canoe. He was surrounded. Escape was impossible. His only hope was that these were a company of fur traders and not part of the British fleet that Lieutenant Hanks had sent him to scout.

"Ahoy! Who goes there?" came the call from a man with a British accent. Although the sound was from a distance, Dousman could tell it was from a much higher vantage point. His heart sank when he turned to face the Englishman. A full orange moon had now completely hatched from its nesting place on the eastern horizon. It clearly revealed a tall ship no more than twenty yards away. Dousman stared in stunned silence as he noted not only the three-masted schooner but also a huge fleet of Indian canoes and Frenchmen's bateaux.

"I say," the man called from the ship. "State your business!"

Michael Dousman recognized the voice. It sounded strange, booming out over the vessel's railing, but it was that of a man he readily knew from his fur trade dealings on St. Joseph's Island. It was the fort's commander, Captain Charles Roberts. Dousman knew at once that he had run headfirst into the British attack force. Lieutenant Hanks was right. War must have been declared. Fort Michilimackinac would be attacked the next morning.

-　　-　　-　　-　　-

In the bowels of the *Caledonia*, eye level with the canoes and bateaux just outside their cell, four American prisoners shared two portholes—eight eyes glued to the drama taking place only a few feet away.

CHAPTER 22
A NEW PRISONER COMES ABOARD

As Michael Dousman regarded the enormous fleet, he realized that Fort Michilimackinac could not withstand the onslaught of such a large attack force. Even if he could warn Lieutenant Hanks, the small garrison would be overwhelmed. When that massacre was done, the townspeople—even his wife, son and daughter at the farm—would be sent swiftly to their deaths. A sudden chill gripped him as he recognized that everything he had worked for and everyone he held dear would soon be destroyed.

To keep that from happening, he must first save his own life. In the pale light, he could see that the Indians were wearing war paint. He knew how they treated their enemies when on the warpath. Tribesmen were known to scalp and kill their conquered foes, cutting off heads, arms and legs on the spot. He understood their belief, that during an enemy's afterlife, the victim could return to haunt his killer. Dismembering the body and scattering its parts to the four winds was the only way to prevent that. The ritual was practiced in many places around the world. Stories of such grisly acts abounded in England, Scotland—all over the globe, but Dousman's concern at the moment was how his captors would treat *him*.

As boats filled with braves surrounded his canoe, the bearded Islander was sure he was about to find out firsthand. A canoe bumped his birchbark craft, tipping it dangerously to one side. Dousman turned to the

161

war-painted Indian and saw the man's face was streaked with blue clay. The brave held a footlong knife over his head, ready to drive it into Dousman's chest. In the same canoe were Ojeeg and Leelinau, the Sioux chief's red-haired nephew and niece. Their father was aboard the *Caledonia* with Captain Roberts.

From the deck of the tall ship, the British commander's voice boomed, "Hold, Red Thunder! Sir, state your business!"

The blue-streaked Indian paused but held his knife at the ready. The Islander turned in his seat and faced the ship. "Captain Roberts, I am Michael Dousman of Mackinac Island," he shouted frantically.

-    -   -   -   -

"That's him!" Dan whispered excitedly from his porthole. "Michael Dousman's the guy Mr. Porter told us about! He's the one in Pete's book!"

"Shh," Kate whispered. "They'll hear us."

-    -   -   -   -

"I am on my way to St. Joseph's Island to see about a shipment of pelts!" Dousman continued. He knew there was no sense lying about that. It was the reason he had been chosen for the mission. Besides, probably half the people who surrounded him, certainly the French voyageurs and many of the Indians, could verify that fact. He had met the British captain many times, although not always on friendly terms, but he hoped for mercy now.

"The white man lies!" the blue-faced Indian exclaimed. "I can see it in his eyes. If we let him go, he will warn the Long Knives at Mishen Imokinakog. We must kill him now, or he will cause us to be killed later!"

A horrible, blood-chilling shout of agreement rose from the surrounding tribesmen. Dark, wildly painted faces pressed ever closer as other canoes jostled his. The bearded Islander stared at the schooner, hoping that the British captain would quiet the angry Indians.

"Bring him aboard," ordered Captain Roberts.

Red Thunder, whose knife was still poised for the deathblow, glared at the man in the tall ship.

"Skaggs! Drop the boarding ladder!" the British officer shouted. "Draw Mr. Dousman up at once!"

Skaggs tossed one end of a climbing rope over the ship's railing. Dousman scrambled as fast as he could from his canoe up to the *Caledonia*'s main deck. He stood before the British commander.

"Take him away, Skaggs!" Captain Roberts bellowed. "Get him some bedding and lock him with the other Americans. Only when Michilimackinac is ours will any of them see light of day." His voice rang out so loudly that all aboard could hear, even the four captives in the prison quarters. Roberts turned to the *Caledonia*'s master. "Sail on, Moneypenny!" he called.

"Set the course!" the ship's master shouted to his first mate.

Sergeant Skaggs pulled his bayonet from its sheath and smirked insolently at his new prisoner. "I'll take you to the ship's store; then it's on to the brig with you!" he said, his voice squeaking. He pushed Dousman along the deck and down one flight of stairs. He stopped at the supply room and signed out a hammock. Mr. Farnsworth duly noted the transaction in his gilt-edged book. Then, along another stairway, they proceeded to the bow. Skaggs undid the padlock and shoved his captive into the compartment with Dan, Kate, Pete and Will. Dousman, holding his hammock, stood before the four Americans. Bright moonlight from the two portholes glimmered upon their faces.

Kate turned to Dan. "It's got to be him," she said.

"Who's got to be who?" Dousman growled angrily.

"You're Mr. Dousman," Kate said, unperturbed by the Islander's bluster.

"Suppose I am," he replied. "What's it to you?"

"Well, Mr. Dousman," Dan began slowly, "we think we have come a very long way to help you."

"Then where were you a few minutes ago?" Dousman growled. "They nearly butchered me out there. Who are you, anyway?"

"We are Americans taken prisoner two days ago," Dan said calmly. "I am Dan Hinken and this is my sister, Kate. Pete Jenkins, here, is a friend, and this is Will Drake."

"You say you're here to help me," Dousman said, sounding a little more civil. "What are you talking about?"

Dan turned to the bearded man. "It's hard to explain without telling you the whole story, but where we come from, you are credited for saving Fort Mackinac after the British attack. We think that we're here to help you do it," he replied flatly.

"And just *where* do you come from?" Dousman asked. "You make it sound as if Mackinac has already been taken."

"For us, it has," Kate answered. She looked at her brother and then at Pete and Will. "We'd better tell him everything," she said.

"You're right," Pete agreed. "He's got to know

sometime."

"None of you are making any sense!" Dousman
sputtered.

"Let me explain," Will said. He faced the Islander.
"You may find this hard to believe, sir," he began, "but
Kate, Dan and Pete have come here from the future to
keep something from happening—something that would
affect me and perhaps many others. You see, Pete, here,
is my great-great-great-grandson!"

At that, Dousman scoffed, staring from face to face of
the two boys who appeared to be within a year of the
same age. "See here!" he snapped. "I will not be
mocked. I don't know what your game is, but if Captain
Roberts has put you up to some devilish scheme, you
can be assured that I am not about to be taken into it."

"You've got to listen to us," Kate pleaded.

"Oh, man! I remember now," Dan nearly shouted.
"Mr. Porter said that after Michael Dousman was caught
by the British near Goose Island, he was brought back
to Mackinac." He stared earnestly at the new prisoner.
"Mr. Dousman, what do you think would happen to the
village after the British soldiers take the fort?"

"To the victors go the spoils," Mr. Dousman said
bluntly. "They clean out what they want from the
enemy camp and, if there's a village nearby, they burn
and steal and kill as they please."

"Then that's it!" Dan said. "Somehow you stop that
from happening. You are the one who takes the
villagers to a safe place." Dan turned to the others.
"Look, guys, I don't remember all the details, but I *do*
know it doesn't happen without Mr. Dousman's help.
That must be why we're here—to get him out of this
cell before the British attack. I don't think we can stop
them from taking over the fort, but maybe we can

165

tweak the *way* it happens."

"Well, you're right about the British attack," Dousman said. "We'll be on the Island before sunrise."

"Three a.m., to be exact," Dan said. "I remember *that* now, too."

"Yes," Dousman said, "four or five hours would be about right." He shook his head as he stared at the four young strangers. "How you could know all this is beyond me, but you still haven't convinced me about coming here from some other time."

Dan turned to his sister. "Kate, show him your jacket." Kate went to the corner, pulled her yellow jacket from under the old sail, and handed it to Mr. Dousman. "Feel it," Dan said. "It's nylon—lighter than any cloth you've ever touched—yet it's tough as iron. Go ahead, try to tear it."

Dousman felt the jacket. "This flimsy thing?" he scoffed. He touched the collar. The brawny man took one sleeve in each of his mammoth hands and snapped the paper-thin garment, expecting it to rip to shreds. It did not. He stared at the jacket and tried even harder. Once again, it showed not even the slightest tear. Dousman looked in surprise at his fellow captives. "This is hardly proof that you can travel through time, but let's say that I am now listening. What is my role in this?"

"All right, then," Kate said eagerly. "Forget *when* we're from. Let's just say that somehow we know what's about to happen. We heard Captain Roberts say that none of us would see light of day until after the fort is taken. Since you can't warn anyone from down here, then we have to do something to get you out."

"I'm all for trying," Dousman said. "My family and farm are there. If there's any way I can save them, I'll

166

do it, but I doubt this door is going to unlock itself."
He grabbed the grated opening and shook it.

It didn't budge.

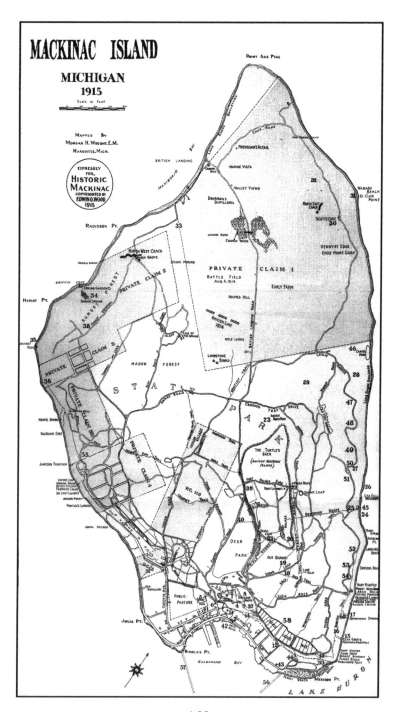

168

CHAPTER 23
THE ISLANDER LEARNS HIS ROLE

Michael Dousman slumped back and sat on his hammock. "It's been a long day," he sighed, "and being locked in the hold of a British ship is not how I would have wished it to end. Still, I'm afraid there is little we can do about it."

"No, sir!" Kate said. "But somehow we *will* get you out!"

"Perhaps," Dousman said, "but as you can see, the locks are strong and the hasps secure. If we are to unlock this door, we must forge the key with our own hands—or minds. Until then, I suggest we rest."

As he said this, a light appeared at the door. With it came a rattling of keys. Skaggs poked his narrow head through the bars. "Present yourself for inspection," he ordered, glancing around the room. "One, two, three, four, five," he said, counting each head. "All prisoners present and accounted for." He pulled his head back from the barred door.

"Sergeant Skaggs," Dan called into the flickering light, "we must speak with Captain Roberts! It's urgent!"

"I doubt the skipper would find it so," Skaggs replied.

"The lives of many people are at stake!" Kate pleaded.

"That is not my concern," Skaggs said. "I'm here to make sure you are where you are supposed to be—and you are. Good night." He turned and began to walk away.

"My young man!" Dousman thundered. He approached the door and glared through the hole after the retreating British soldier. "You *will* speak with me!"

Skaggs whirled and faced his newest prisoner. "What was that?" he said indignantly. Even in the darkness, Pete could sense Skaggs' face reddening. "First, I am not 'Your young man.' I am *Sergeant* Skaggs! And second, you are in no position to be giving orders!"

"You must allow me to speak to Captain Roberts," Dousman insisted. "I am a militia captain. By the protocol of rank, I am allowed a word with my senior captor!"

"You are *allowed* nothing in the state of war!" Skaggs barked. "The captain is busy. Such business as you may have with him will have to wait until such time as he wishes to address you!"

"What I have to say cannot wait," Dousman asserted. "It is of utmost importance."

"It *can* and *will* wait, sir!" Skaggs said with an emphatic chirp. He turned and disappeared down the long hallway. The prisoners were once again cast into the darkness of their moving jail as the *Caledonia* plowed through the waves westward toward Fort Michilimackinac.

"I'm more convinced now than ever that this is why we're here," Dan said. "We've got to find a way to get Mr. Dousman up on deck to speak with Captain Roberts."

"How are we going to do that?" Will asked. "I doubt if Skaggs or anyone will check on us again until after it's too late."

Dousman faced the others. "If your fantastic story is to be believed," he spoke slowly, "we shall be arriving in less than four hours. Perhaps we will have another chance then. If we are to do what you say, we will need our strength. For that reason, we had better get some sleep."

Everyone agreed and stretched out in their hammocks—everyone except Pete. Pete stared for a moment at the door and then picked up Kate's yellow jacket. He began to twist it into a short rope. "I think Mr. Dousman's right," he said. "We'll have to look for our chance and, when it comes, be ready." He then went to his hammock and settled in.

The steady pounding of the rolling seas against *Caledonia*'s hull swung the prisoners' beds gently. From aloft came the hypnotic droning of the fresh breeze as it whistled through the ship's rigging. The combination soon put the five Americans into a deep sleep.

-　　-　　-　　-　　-

Suddenly, Pete awakened. All was silent. The waves' rhythmic pounding on the *Caledonia*'s hull had stopped. A strong scent of cedar wafted through the portholes into the prisoners' cell. Pete guessed that the British vessel had arrived at Mackinac Island, so he rolled from his hammock and moved across the deck to the nearest porthole.

He peered outside and saw the silver setting. The brilliant moon and stars vividly disclosed the fleet of Canadian bateaux and Indian canoes. The oarsmen and passengers sat quietly in their craft, silently awaiting Captain Roberts' orders. Beyond them, in the gray light, Pete saw the unmistakable silhouette of Mackinac Island. He knew exactly where he was—a place called British Landing, named and known forever after for the very reason they were there now. Pete watched a heavy cannon being lowered from the deck onto a sturdy boat.

"Dan, Kate!" Pete whispered, tugging each of his friends' shoulders. "We're at Mackinac! Will! Mr. Dousman! Wake up!"

Dan jumped to his feet and rushed to the porthole. "We have to get out of here!" he said anxiously.

"But how?" Kate asked.

Pete was distracted by a sound in the hallway. He hurried to the door and peeked through the opening. "We just need one break," he whispered, "and I think we're about to get it."

"What do you mean?" Kate asked.

"No time to explain," Pete said softly. "Just don't let on that you know where I am."

The others glanced quickly at each other, and before anyone could say anything, from outside the door a flame flickered—a flame both of light and of hope. Footsteps were approaching. Pete wished—no, he *prayed*—that it would be Skaggs. He grabbed Kate's yellow jacket. Winding it into a tight coil, he knelt at the side of the door. A moment later the ferret-faced soldier appeared.

CHAPTER 24
A SURPRISE FOR SKAGGS

"There you are," Skaggs said, laughing through the grate into his captives' faces. "Soon, Michilimackinac will be ours. When it is, I will lead you to the village where you will receive the same reward as the other Yankee traitors!"

He poked his nose between the iron bars. Holding the lantern beside his head, he searched the room. He squeezed his face farther inside and scanned the cell's corners. He glanced in all directions, forcing the light closer as if something was amiss. He wiggled farther inside, his head and neck now completely through the bars. "Someone's not here!" he shouted. "Hey! Where's that skinny kid?"

From the floor, Pete looked straight up. Leaping to his feet, he faced the startled soldier. "Right here!" he said. In one motion, he swung the crude nylon rope over Skaggs' head and twisted it around his neck. With one hand on each jacket sleeve, Pete pulled Skaggs' shoulders hard against the hole. "Now!" Pete shouted. "Unlock this door!"

As the lantern flickered, Skaggs tried to scream for help, but with Pete's stranglehold, he barely made a sound. Skaggs struggled mightily to free himself, jerking his head, squirming his body, and flailing his arms—all to no avail. Pete's grip and the nylon material held.

"Pete! You're going to break his neck!" Kate screamed. Her warning served more to terrify Skaggs than deter Pete.

"Fine by me," Pete replied with a grunt. "He'd better unlock it while he still can!"

At that, there was a frantic jangling of keys. Soon, the dead bolt moved in the lock. Dan pulled the door toward him with Skaggs still pinned to it. Kate grabbed the keys from Skaggs' hand. "What are we going to do with him?" she asked.

"We'll lock him here," Dan said.

"But he'll call for help through the portholes," Kate warned.

"We'll have to gag him," Pete said.

Dan pulled Skaggs' shoes from his feet and tossed them into a corner. He then yanked off his long stockings. One he stuffed in the soldier's mouth and the other he used to tie Skaggs' hands and feet together.

"We'll lock the door and tie him to it," Dan said, knotting the gag in place.

Pete unhooked his hammock and wrapped Skaggs in it. Then, using the yellow jacket, he secured Skaggs to the door. The British soldier was stuck like a rat in a trap. "That should hold him," Pete said, putting one last knot to Skaggs' squirming feet. "Let's get up top."

Following Kate, who held the lantern, the three boys and Michael Dousman hurried to the main deck. There, they found Captain Roberts about to descend the ladder into an awaiting bateau. Pete led the others across the deck and up to the British commander. "Captain Roberts!" he called out.

The officer turned quickly and faced the five Americans. "What in the . . .! How did you get here?" he demanded.

"We told Sergeant Skaggs that we needed to speak with you," Kate managed to answer with a straight face.

"Where is he now?" the captain shouted. He looked about the deck.

"I'm sure he's helping with the sails," Pete answered. "He told us to go on without him."

Just then Michael Dousman stepped in front of the others. "Captain Roberts," he said. "We fear for the villagers' lives. Please allow me to take them to a safe place."

The British commander stared at the bearded Islander. "I can't do that," he replied. "The element of surprise is key to my attack."

"You know as well as I," Dousman implored, "that once firing commences, your forces will not stop at laying waste to the fort. They will storm the village as well. Many of your troops do not make the distinction between American soldiers and American citizens. They despise them all. They will set fire to the village and massacre everyone."

"I cannot change that," Captain Roberts said. "If that is their will, then so be it."

"But you cannot allow so many innocent women and children to be killed," Dousman implored. "I know these people. Yes, some are American patriots, but many others remain loyal to the King. You would let *them* die? Also remember, as commander of the fort, you will need the services of the townspeople. Your soldiers are not farmers or blacksmiths. They are not harness makers or carpenters. Who will repair the fort when you are in charge? Who will raise crops to feed your soldiers and fashion shoes for your horses?"

"It is out of the question," Captain Roberts said, waving his hand in dismissal. "I cannot take the chance that someone would alert Lieutenant Hanks."

"And what if they did?" Dousman argued. "You have

a thousand men and a cannon. Lieutenant Hanks has fifty soldiers. By the time we have led the villagers to safety, you will be in position to take Fort Michilimackinac. Look, I know for a fact that it will be yours by noon."

Captain Roberts stared for a moment at Dousman. "How could you possibly know that?"

Dousman replied grimly, "Let's just say I have inside information."

"Your source must be able to see into the future," Captain Roberts said in a cynical tone.

Pete whispered to Kate, "Or travel into the past."

"As I said, my source is reliable," Dousman said.

Captain Roberts leveled his gaze at Dousman. "You would not pass word to even one soldier?" he said, squaring his shoulders to the Islander. "I have your word as a gentleman?"

"You do, sir," Michael Dousman answered.

"I wish I could tell you that I have such control over the various tribesmen that have accompanied me in this attack. They often do as their chiefs tell them. The chiefs often consult their own men in such matters," Roberts said, shaking his head. "It would be unheard-of for them to consider such a request. Still, I will allow you ashore. I warn you, however, that if one shot is fired in the defense of the fort—just one—you will be responsible for whatever follows."

"Agreed," Mr. Dousman said. He paused and spoke, "I would ask for the use of the ship's longboat and the help of my American friends. I will need them in the village to spread the word."

Captain Roberts looked at the four captives. "I will allow three of them to assist you. One I must take with me to ensure the return of the others. If anything goes wrong, I will not vouch for his safety."

Mr. Dousman nodded. "Understood," he said. He turned to Dan, Kate, Pete and Will. "Do I have a volunteer to remain with Captain Roberts?"

The four glanced nervously at each other. Pete now felt responsible for getting them all into this jam. He stepped forward, "I will," he said.

"Then it is agreed," Captain Roberts said. "You others must return to the *Caledonia* when your job is done."

The ship's bell rang with three double chimes, six bells on the graveyard watch—three a.m. One by one, Dan, Will, Kate and finally Mr. Dousman stepped down the rope ladder from the *Caledonia* into a long, narrow rowboat. Pete remained at the captain's side until they, too, boarded another shore boat loaded with British soldiers. As they passed the *Caledonia*'s bow, Pete heard the muffled sounds below decks of Skaggs thrashing about, still trying to free himself from his bindings.

CHAPTER 25
THE ROW INTO TOWN
AND AN EXPLANATION

Kate, Dan and Will readied their oars for the three-mile row. With their backs to their destination, they anxiously awaited the call from their coxswain, Michael Dousman, as he settled himself in the stern.

"Hurry, Mr. Dousman," Kate whispered. "If Skaggs gets free, he'll tell Roberts what happened, and we'll have to go back aboard."

The Islander nodded and then called to Captain Roberts, who sat with Pete in a shore launch. "I'll direct the people to the distillery just west of town," Dousman said. "Send a guard there. The villagers will need protection from each other as much as from your troops."

Roberts signaled with a wave. "You'd better not try any tricks, Dousman. Remember, I've got a hostage who will lead our attack if there's any gunfire from the fort!"

Kate, from her seat closest to Mr. Dousman, asked, "What does he mean by that?"

Dousman hesitated. He then replied, "If Roberts thinks I've double-crossed him, he'll send Pete in the first charge. He'll be gunned down by the Americans as easily as if he were a standing target on a firing range."

Kate looked horrified. "You think he means it?" she gasped. The thought of Pete being used as a pawn in this deadly game put a terrifying slant on the whole plan.

"I *know* he means it," Dousman replied. "Roberts is

worried that I might warn Lieutenant Hanks and give him time to prepare a defense. Now, *I* know Hanks could not possibly move even one cannon in so short a time, but Captain Roberts doesn't know it. And even if Hanks could, it would hold off the British for only a day or two. Roberts has too large a force. He's got the Americans outnumbered by over ten to one. But I know Hanks. If I *did* warn him, he'd fight to the finish, and the result would be complete devastation. That's why we've got to convince the villagers to go straight to the distillery without leaking word to the fort."

"Then let's get rowing!" Will said grimly.

Dousman looked ahead toward town, cupped his hands to his mouth and said to his oarsmen, "On my signal. Ready. Stroke!" In unison, Dan, Kate and Will brought the six oars toward the bow, dipped them into the dark Straits water, then pulled them with all their might toward the stern. After a momentary rest, Dousman again called, "Stroke!"

Pull after pull, the small boat moved along the calm waters. "Stroke . . . Stroke . . . Stroke," Dousman breathed quietly in the moonlight. It was 3:30. Dawn was still hours away.

As the three oarsmen fell into a regular rhythm, Kate leaned closer to Dousman and asked, "What will be so hard about getting the villagers to go to a safe place?"

"Some will not be easily convinced to keep quiet about the British attack," Dousman answered. "There are strong feelings on all sides about what we will be telling them."

"What *sides* do you mean?" Dan asked. "All the people of Mackinac Island are Americans, aren't they?"

Will Drake answered for Mr. Dousman. "Yes," he said grimly, "but those 'Americans' have come from many places. France, England, and Ireland, mainly. Also, several Indian tribes live here. Hatred between some of them goes back centuries. My father warned me that life on Mackinac Island would be very tense. He told me I'd have to watch every word I said to keep from offending one group or another."

"Your father was right," Dousman said. "Everyone here knows they need to get along to survive, but that doesn't mean they have to *like* each other. Englishmen hate the French, Irish hate the English, Indians hate the Americans—emotions among them simmer constantly. It stays under the boiling point only so long as rivals keep their distance. Somehow, we must gather all those people under one roof and still keep them apart."

"It's hard to imagine that there is so much hatred in such a small place," Kate said. "Our island in the Snows is much larger than Mackinac, and nothing like that ever happened there."

"This island is very different," Dousman said. "As small as it may seem, its location in the Straits makes any ship going to any other part of the upper lakes visible from the fort and vulnerable to attack. The nation that holds Fort Michilimackinac controls the destiny of a vast territory. Many of the Americans living here can tell horror stories of being attacked by the British during the Revolution. They will be outraged at the thought of being the King's subjects once again."

The four rowed along the shoreline under the Island's West Bluff, where one day magnificent summer homes would overlook the Straits. Soon, the land began to slope downward toward town. The rowboat was nearing Biddle Point, the very southern tip of Mackinac Island. In Dan and Kate's time, it was a place where hotels, shops, bicycles, horse-drawn carriages and thousands of tourists would abound every summer day, but now the silvery light exposed nothing but silhouettes of a few small shacks, teepees and wigwams along the shoreline. The *Caldonia*'s long boat moved around the point and silently into Haldimand Bay.

"We'll land there," Mr. Dousman said, pointing ahead. It was a place Dan and Kate knew as Lakeview Hotel's beach. Mr. Dousman scanned the area for activity, but there was none. It was still an hour before sunrise. A glimmer of light in the east created a ghostly gray aspect to the dwellings and trees.

"Hold your oars," Dousman called softy. The three rowers let the boat coast toward the pebbled shore where it ground to a halt. Dan leaped from the bow, an anchor rope in hand. He hurried to a mooring post and threw a double half hitch around it.

CHAPTER 26
THE GATHERING PLACE

Kate gazed across the horizon. "It's Mackinac Harbor, all right," she said, "but it sure looks strange without all the docks and boats tied up everywhere."

"Right, but there's the fort," Dan said, pointing to the awesome structure in the distance.

"There's a light over there," Will said, nodding toward a wood frame house a short way up the hill.

"That's Sylvester Day's place," Dousman said. "He's the fort surgeon, but he lives in town and treats all the villagers as well. Still, his first allegiance is to the United States Army, so once he hears of the British attack he may take the news to Lieutenant Hanks. I must convince him not to do that."

"Tell us again: Where should we direct the people to go?" Kate asked.

"There's a distillery just west of the village," the Islander replied as he led the way toward the lighted house. "It's big enough for all the people and far enough out of town to serve our purpose. Everyone here knows where it is."

Soon the four approached Dr. Day's house. Dousman knocked quietly at the door. It opened and Dr. Day stared in surprise at the faces of his visitors. "Michael, I thought you were going to St. Joseph's Island," he said.

"I was captured by the British off Goose Island," Dousman replied. "We are at war," he added plainly. He then quickly explained the situation and finished with Captain Roberts' orders. "I will need your help passing the word. As their doctor, the British loyalists will listen

183

to you where they would only slam the door in my face."

Dr. Day paused for a moment, then nodded.

"We will split up," Dousman continued. "Take this young man with you. His name is Will Drake." The Islander turned to Will. "If anything bad should happen, come and get me." At that, Dousman motioned Dan and Kate to follow him.

Sylvester Day stepped back into his house and grabbed a coat and hat from a nearby rack. He then led Will toward the high ground of Market Street and pointed to the homes they needed to call upon. They worked together, stopping at all the British sympathizers' houses. Will noticed the mixed emotions of joy and concern that the news brought.

Finally, Dr. Day turned to Will. "I've got one place I have to go. You can handle this next one yourself," he said, pointing to a fine house at the end of Market Street. "It's your last stop. You know what to tell them. I'll meet you at the distillery." At that, Dr. Day turned and hurried up a hill.

Will moved quickly to the house and rapped on the door. In a few moments, he was staring into the face of the prettiest girl he had ever seen. "I-I am Will Drake," he stammered. "I am here as a messenger from Dr. Day. The British are about to attack the fort, and he says for everyone to go at once to the distillery. To be honest, I don't know where it is myself."

At first, the girl seemed shocked, but then she nodded. "I'm Averill Newcastle," she said pleasantly. "I will tell my parents and brother. Stay here for a moment, and you can come with us."

It was 7 a.m. by the time Will, Averill and her family arrived at the meeting place. Already, a British soldier

Averill Newcastle

was stationed at the door. Just then, Michael Dousman, Dan and Kate approached from another direction. Together, they all went inside. A hundred people in various stages and forms of dress—from nightshirts to day clothes—were milling about. Pete noticed that many were squabbling heatedly, while others simply stood in small groups, glaring at other small groups. When the villagers saw Dousman, the shouting began.

"What's this all about, Michael?" a man called out.

Dousman raised a hand. "As we have told you, Britain and the United States are at war," he said firmly. "For your protection from the attacking army, the British captain has allowed me to warn you and direct you to a safe place. He made me promise not to reveal this to anyone at the fort."

"Where are these British soldiers?" another demanded.

"They are marching up from the back of the Island," Dousman said. "They landed at three a.m. and must be near the north wall by now."

"How many are there?" demanded another angry villager.

"Captain Roberts has only fifty British soldiers, but he commands a force of nearly a thousand Indian warriors and French-Canadian woodsmen," Dousman replied.

"A thousand!" a woman cried. "What will stop them from coming into the village? They will loot and burn until nothing is left."

"That is why we are here," Dousman explained. "I was able to convince Captain Roberts to spare your lives. He agreed that you would be safer here away from the village than in your homes where you would have no protection at all."

A man hollered, "Our lives may be spared, but only to return to a burned-out village! Is that what you're telling us?"

"Better that than to watch your wives and children die before your eyes," Dousman replied. "With life, there is hope. We can always rebuild."

"I will never live again under English law!" a man yelled, raising his fists.

A British loyalist standing across the room shouted, "Now you will find what it is to be treated as a foreigner in your own village!"

"I would rather die fighting than live once again under that murdering tyrant," the first man argued. "I say we go to the fort and warn Lieutenant Hanks!"

Just then Dr. Day entered the door and came to Dousman's side.

"Where have you been?" Dousman asked. "I was afraid something had happened to you when I saw Will return and you were not with him."

"I went up to the fort to alert my superior officer," the doctor said.

Dousman stared at the doctor in horror. "You what?" he asked.

"I went to Lieutenant Hanks to explain what was happening," Dr. Day replied calmly. "But I couldn't do it. I know him. He would have done everything in his power to move cannon, shot and shell into place to defend the fort. Every soldier would have died, and it would have been my fault. At least, if Hanks is surprised—taken completely unaware—there is a glimmer of hope that a truce can be made."

"That is true," Dousman said. "It is not something I had thought of. I will go now to Roberts and plead for him to consider a peaceful treaty."

Kate and Dan stood nearby, listening to the two men. Suddenly, they faced each other, whispering. Finally, Kate grabbed Dousman's arm. "Excuse me," she said, pulling him to the side. "Dan and I have another idea."

"What is it?" Dousman asked.

Kate whispered, "It's sort of in between what Doctor Day was *going* to do and what you are now suggesting that you *should* do. In our time it's called a bluff."

"I'm familiar with the term," Dousman said. "I just don't know what you intend."

Kate leaned closer to the Islander and explained.

A slow smile crossed Dousman's face. "Brilliant!" he exclaimed. He turned to the door. "I have no time to lose."

"Kate and I are coming, too," Dan said.

Dousman glanced at Will. "Stay here with Dr. Day and help keep the peace," he said. Then he faced the agitated villagers. "Please, for everyone's sake, stay here and remain calm until we return."

It was 9:15 when Dousman, Dan and Kate left the distillery.

A strained silence fell upon the anxious gathering. People of the various factions moved apart and talked fearfully among themselves. Meanwhile, the British sentry kept guard at the door.

Then, at exactly ten a.m., a thunderous cannon blast shook the Island.

There was a momentary calm as the boom echoed throughout the Straits. It was quickly followed within the distillery by angry shouts, which rose to a deafening pitch. Villagers began to shove and push their neighbors.

"It has begun!" Averill Newcastle said, grabbing Will's hand. She looked fearfully into his eyes.

He responded by taking her other hand in his.

"Perhaps it has," he said, facing her. "But if I know my friends, that blast may simply be the signal that it is over."

About To Fire On Fort

CHAPTER 27
MEANWHILE, AT BRITISH LANDING, PETE HIKES WITH THE ENEMY

It was just after three a.m. The moon, now high in the sky, gave silvery light to the shoreline on the northwest shore of Mackinac Island. The British troops stood patiently awaiting Captain Roberts' instructions.

Pete sat beside the British commander as four soldiers rowed them from the *Caledonia* to shore. In the distance, he heard Mr. Dousman calling rowing orders to Dan, Kate and Will as they moved away in their longboat toward the village.

It was the first time in this whole strange visit into the past that Pete had not been with someone from his own time. He felt very alone.

"Bring the cannon ashore," Captain Roberts said to his troops. "I will need four teams of eight men to carry it up to the high ground. Everyone else, go before them and clear a path with your axes!" At once, thirty-two of the sturdiest voyageurs came to Roberts' side while the rest of the English, Canadian and Indian men jumped into the dense underbrush with whatever hatchets and axes they had. With so many workers, a wide swath was quickly carved up the steep hill.

Pete watched as the first team of brawny men hauled the cannon from the bateau onto the beach. The weight of the artillery piece strained their muscles until, exhausted, they set it down.

The next group jumped forward and hoisted the unwieldy hunk of iron a few paces up the sharp incline. No sooner had they run out of steam then the next unit stepped in to take their place. Before long, the four teams had taken the weapon to the Island's crest.

It was five a.m. The sun was about to rise, and the troops no longer needed the moon to see the terrain.

"Just beyond here is a road," Captain Roberts said. "A farm is nearby. I'm sure we will find a wagon there to move it the rest of the way."

As the men made the final pull through the cleared path, Pete stood beside the British officer. "How can you be sure about the road, the farm and the wagon?" he asked.

"Sixteen years ago Michilimackinac was a British fort," Captain Roberts said. "I have a map of the Island from when it was ours. Change comes slowly to such remote outposts. I have faith that much is the same as it was before we left."

True enough, once they reached level ground, Pete saw a plowed field and a barn nearby. Inside, there stood a small wagon. The Canadian men ran to it and hoisted the cannon onto its bed. In another stall stood a draught horse. They harnessed it quickly, and from there they led it two miles over a narrow, two-track road. By seven a.m. they had come to another more gradual hill. It led to a place called Turtle Back, the very highest point of Mackinac Island.

Captain Roberts, rather than ordering his men up that hill, had them bring the cannon as silently as possible to a position not as high, but closer to the fort's north gate. From there, the gun still held a commanding view over the fort wall.

The sun was now an intense, gleaming ball of red. The mid-July morning was already uncomfortably warm. By 9:30, Captain Roberts was in the final stages of his plan. He ordered the cannon to be placed at the edge of a stand of trees not more than three hundred yards from the fort. He pointed the muzzle above the wall into the parade grounds.

It was nearly ten a.m. by the time everyone was in place. Captain Roberts gazed across the sunbaked field between his position and the fort. It was an area that long ago had been cleared by soldiers to deprive an advancing enemy of shielded access to the walls. Riflemen standing along the rampart would have no trouble picking off any normal enemy attack.

But *this* would be no normal attack. With the first cannon blast, the thousand British troops would storm the fort, scale the walls and overwhelm the small garrison. The American soldiers would never know what hit them. Even if they could get into position to return fire, they would not be able to reload and shoot quickly enough to withstand the swarming enemy. They would be massacred. There would, of course, be a few casualties among Roberts' troops, but that was to be expected in war.

Once the fort was secured, the remaining attackers, with fire in their eyes, would do as they pleased to the town, ransacking, pillaging, looting and burning. For the civilians' sake, the British captain hoped Dousman had been successful in moving the Islanders to a safe place, but even so, their lives could not be guaranteed.

-     -   -   -   -

Pete stood nervously at Captain Roberts' side. Several times during the long hike he had felt the urge to bolt and run away. But every time he thought about it, he stopped, not knowing where he might bolt *to*. Now he was staring at the fort's immense north wall. Only three days before, and in another time, he had stood on this exact spot with Dan and Kate, who had been telling him odd bits of trivia about the War of 1812. At the time, their stories had seemed unimportant—ancient history. Now it was all *too* important. Just ahead, he noticed one small pine growing only a few feet from the north sally port. Could this be the seedling that would grow to be the tree that he, Kate and Dan had used to catapult themselves into the fort? It seemed so long ago, but in fact, it was 140 years into the future.

-    -   -   -   -

As Captain Roberts ordered the Royal Artillery's sergeant and two gunners to prepare the cannon for firing, Pete noticed three people running up the hill from town. It was Michael Dousman with Dan and Kate right behind him.

Dousman waved anxiously to Captain Roberts. "Hold it! Don't fire!" he shouted.

Captain Roberts faced the Islander. "What is it, Dousman?" he said in annoyance.

"I need a word with you." Dousman was breathing heavily. "It is urgent. We have come in hopes that a truce can be made," Dousman said urgently.

"A truce!" Roberts exclaimed. "A truce implies compromise. I'm holding all the aces. Why should I offer a truce?"

"Word of the attack has leaked to the fort," Dousman said, catching his breath. "I believe Lieutenant Hanks has had time to move his 24- and 32-pound heavy cannon into position to batter your positions. But I doubt he knows the size of your army. In the end, his attempt would be futile, but many of your men would undoubtedly be killed. It would be a bloody affair for both sides. You must allow me to convince him that his efforts would result in the loss of his entire regiment."

Captain Roberts looked caustically at the Islander.

"How do I know this is true?"

"I just saw Dr. Day," Mr. Dousman said. "He told me that, after helping me bring the civilians to safety, he felt it his duty to tell Hanks where you were going to attack. I hadn't had time to tell him how many men were in your force, so he may have told Hanks that you have come only with your own small garrison."

"He will learn soon enough," Roberts said, raising his hand to the artillery sergeant. "Hanks' regiment will have no answer for my army."

"You and I know it," Dousman said, "but *he* doesn't know it. And I know Hanks. Once firing commences, he will fight to the end. Can you risk the deaths of so many of your own men? You must allow me to request a truce."

"How do I know you would represent me well?" the British officer asked.

"We came here from town of our own free will," Mr. Dousman replied. "We would have no reason to tell Lieutenant Hanks otherwise. You have my word as a gentleman."

"I had your word that you would not warn the fort, and you failed me," Captain Roberts said, narrowing his eyes at the American. "Be assured that I *will* keep *my* word should any gunfire come from the fort." He reached over and grabbed Pete's arm. "My hostage here will face what would amount to an American firing squad should he lead my men into battle."

"Let me approach the fort under a white flag," Dousman said, "I will apprise Lieutenant Hanks of your numbers and suggest he consider a deal. What harm can come of that?"

Captain Roberts stared grimly. He looked at the fort, its impenetrable walls, and considered the possibility that powerful artillery—weapons much heavier than his six-pound field cannon—were in place to repel his attack. Finally, he nodded. "There is merit to what you say," he said. "All right, we will announce our presence with a blank round from the cannon. You may then advance upon the fort under a white flag. You will carry my written conditions for surrender." He nodded to the gunner, who was holding an iron ball, and motioned for him to set it on the ground. Roberts then withdrew a parchment sheet from a leather carrying case at his side. He inked a quill and began to write. In two minutes he handed the message to Dousman.

Dousman scanned the document. "I will deliver it as you wish," he said. "I suggest that before you send me, you place your troops in positions that will be visible to Lieutenant Hanks. As I will be telling him of your large force, he will need to see evidence of it."

"Your suggestion is a good one, Dousman," Captain Roberts said. He turned to the man nearest the cannon. "Sergeant, prepare to fire a blank round!"

The Royal Artillery sergeant rammed the batting into the barrel, leaving the six-pound iron ball on the ground. He then poured a quantity of black gunpowder into the drilled hole. He stood back and held a flint striker nearby.

"Fire!" Captain Roberts ordered. The artilleryman ignited the charge.

CHAPTER 28
TRUCE

At exactly 10 a.m. a thunderous blast sent the cannon recoiling. The report reverberated for several seconds, echoing from every island in the entire Straits area.

A few moments lapsed before Dan, Kate and Pete, from their vantage point high above the fort walls, could see movement inside. American soldiers scrambled in all directions. As they did, the British captain ordered his cannon recharged, this time fully loaded. Pete stared nervously over the wall at the American troops. If they fired back, it would mean certain death for him.

A minute passed. Then two. Pete saw several American soldiers hurry across the courtyard to the north rampart and point their rifles onto the battlefield. But still, there was no return fire.

Captain Roberts made a hand signal to his left and right, signaling to his forces to show themselves and to display their rifles. The Canadian woodsmen and painted Indians stepped from behind every tree and rock, waving guns, tomahawks and scaling ropes.

There was stillness in both camps, a calm almost . . . but anxiety screamed in Pete's ears.

After five minutes there were still no shots from the American soldiers. Captain Roberts called Dousman to his side. "You may approach the fort," he said. "Take your three Americans with you."

"No hostage?" he asked, glancing at Pete.

197

"No, he's served his time," Roberts said. "Go."

"Right away, sir," Dousman said. He turned to Dan, Kate and Pete. "Ready?"

"Yes, sir," Dan and Kate said at once. Pete also nodded. He was glad to be back with his friends. Still, he knew that British rifles would be trained on his back and American ones aimed at his head as he walked toward the fort. Captain Roberts handed Pete a staff with a small white cloth tied to the top. Down the hill toward the fort the four Americans went, Pete waving the flag as high and as often as he could.

Halfway to the fort, Kate whispered to Pete. "You know, this is all a big bluff," she said.

"What?" Pete asked.

"Hanks had no idea that the British were here and ready to attack," Kate explained. "Dan and I told Mr. Dousman that maybe, from a strong bargaining position, even if it wasn't real, we might be able to make a deal. It was worth a try. I mean, what could happen? Roberts bit and here we are. Now all we have to do is get Hanks to do his part."

Pete shook his head. Is there nothing these two couldn't do? He turned to Kate and asked, "Where's Will?"

"He's at the distillery with Dr. Day and the rest of the Islanders," she answered. "He's safe for the moment, but if we can't pull this off and fighting starts, who knows where it will end. That's why we have to convince Hanks to accept the truce."

Pete realized that a cease-fire would save *him*, but that wouldn't explain why he had come back in time. Wasn't the whole idea to help *Will*? Or *was* it? Who else might be kept alive by this whole event? Pete's brain wasn't feeling particularly nimble just now, but he knew there must be more to his purpose than keeping the British from overrunning the fort. Some*one* or some*thing*—some part of the equation—was missing, but he didn't know who or what.

Slowly, before him, the north gate swung open. Inside stood three men—American officers all, by the looks of their blue uniforms. Pete led the truce party onto the fort grounds with Dousman holding Captain Roberts' document in his right hand. The gate closed behind them.

The bearded Islander's voice was grave as he presented the parchment to Lieutenant Hanks, saying, "I'm sorry that I have not returned under better circumstances, but I was captured near Goose Island. England and the United States are at war. It was declared almost a month ago. Why no one has brought such news to you until it became my unfortunate duty to do so, I cannot say. Only with the help of these young Americans could I have been able to take the villagers to a place of safety. As you no doubt have observed, Captain Roberts has a large force of Canadians, Indians and British soldiers, who would make any defense on your part a grievous mistake. Should you elect to stand and fight, I would, of course, respect your decision and relay your intentions to Captain Roberts. Here are his conditions of surrender."

Lieutenant Hanks took the paper from Dousman and read it.

"In short," Dousman said solemnly, "it says that the United States will give up the fort to Britain. Our troops will be sent to Detroit with the understanding that they will not take up arms for any purpose until the war is over. All American citizens living on the Island will be asked to take an oath of allegiance to Britain within one month. Should they not, they would be forced to leave the Island."

Lieutenant Hanks gazed sadly at Old Glory with its fifteen stars and fifteen stripes floating in the morning breeze. He turned and eyed the hundreds of enemy troops gathered in the fields beyond the fort wall. He sighed deeply. Finally he said, "For the sake of my soldiers who would surely fight to the death if I asked it of them, I must now submit my command and give in to the British Crown."

There was a moment's pause.

"There's one more thing," Dousman said. He smiled at the American lieutenant. "Actually, we have been allowed to approach you only with the help of a very clever ploy."

"A ploy?" Lieutenant Hanks asked incredulously. "This is no time for jokes. What do you mean?"

"Captain Roberts was all set to charge your fort without any warning," Dousman said, "but these two young Americans devised a plan to stop him." He turned to Dan and Kate and said, "I believe, since you two are the designers of this little stratagem, that you should be the ones to explain it to the lieutenant."

"Yes, sir," Kate said. She faced the American commander. "We have told Captain Roberts that news of the attack has come to you during the night."

Hanks looked mystified. "But that's not true," he said.

Dan continued, "We told Captain Roberts that you have had time to move two of your cannon into position and are able to defend the north wall. He is convinced that you have a 24- and a 32-pounder ready to return fire."

"It would have taken me several days to do *that*," Hanks scoffed.

"*You* know that," Kate said, "but *he* doesn't know that."

Hanks turned to Dousman and asked softly, "You think he'll fall for it?"

"To some degree, he already has," Dousman said. "He was loading his cannon when we stepped in."

Kate said, "We were afraid that, once the attackers battered down the fort walls, there would be nothing to stop them from burning the town."

"Look, Mr. Hanks," Dan said, "if this is going to work, you've got to show Captain Roberts that you are capable of repelling his charge—that you are holding at least some of the aces—even if you're not."

"And those aces are two cannon?" Lieutenant Hanks asked.

"Right," Dan said evenly. "You must tell him that, if you are to give over your fort without a fight, he must assure you of one thing."

"And what *thing* is that?" Hanks asked.

" . . . that no damage will come to the village nor harm to its citizens," Kate said.

Hanks scoffed. "Such a request would be unprecedented," he said, again sensing the futility of the entire situation.

"Ask it anyway," Pete said, stepping from behind the others. "It won't hurt," he added, "and if it works, it would save a lot of people."

Hanks glanced at Dousman. "Do you honestly think we can pull this off?" he asked.

"What do we have to lose?" Dousman replied.

Hanks nodded and took a quill from his pouch. At the bottom of Captain Roberts' terms of surrender, he wrote his amendment. He returned it to Dousman saying, "Tell Captain Roberts that, if not granted, I will instruct my men to pound them with my cannon for as long as we are able to stand."

Dousman smiled at Dan, Kate and Pete, admiration in his eyes. "So noted," he said. The four messengers turned and hiked back through the gate.

CHAPTER 29
THE UNION JACK FLIES OVER
FORT MICHILIMACKINAC

Pete nervously led the truce party up the hill to the British camp, his white flag again held high.

When they reached Captain Roberts, Dousman handed the amended terms to the English officer. "Lieutenant Hanks accepts your offer, under one condition," he said, pointing to the bottom of the page.

Roberts' grim expression didn't change as he read Hanks' clause for surrender.

"If you cannot ensure that," Dousman said, "in writing and signed by yourself on behalf of all the Canadian leaders and the various tribal chiefs, Hanks said he will not quit firing until he gasps his last breath."

Captain Roberts looked troubled for a moment, then muttered, "He surely can't expect me to . . . the men would . . ." He then turned quickly to Mascotapah, the red-haired fur trader. "Mr. Dickson, call your Canadian leaders and tribal chiefs to council!" he ordered.

In ten minutes, twenty men of various races and nationalities gathered around Captain Roberts. He stood beside the cannon, which was now fully loaded and aimed at Fort Michilimackinac's north wall. Warriors from each tribe, including Chief Red Thunder, sat cross-legged in a circle, their stoic expressions revealing none of their thoughts. Red Thunder's red-haired nephew and niece, Ojeeg and Leelinau, joined their Scotsman father, Robert Dickson, as part of the council.

Roberts insisted that the four Americans, Pete, Dan, Kate and Michael Dousman, join the group.

"Today, we will take the first step toward reclaiming this territory for the British Empire," Roberts began. "By seizing Fort Michilimackinac, England's naval fleet will control the upper lakes. Our enemy's supply routes to the west will be broken. Their forts will tumble like dominoes. The entire continent will be ours by the end of the year!"

"*Bon! C'est magnifique!*" cheered the French fur traders. They would once again dominate the vast peltry. Wild whoops of victory spread to the Indian leaders, for they knew the hunting grounds would be theirs as before.

"It is customary," Captain Roberts added, holding a hand up for silence, "that when an army is victorious, its soldiers may take anything they want as spoils of war. It was so in ancient Rome and Britain, just as it is now, here in the wilds of this new continent."

Loud shouts of approval came from around the circle.

"But today," he continued emphatically, "I must ask that you refrain from any such acts. I have learned that the Americans have moved artillery into position and are capable of a strong defense. Even with that, I know we have sufficient advantages to be victorious, but during its course, many of you would die as a result. I see no reason to risk such casualties. The American lieutenant, Mr. Hanks, has agreed to surrender only if no harm comes to the village or its people. I plan to accept his proposal."

Red Thunder jumped to his feet. "How can you ask this!" he exclaimed. "My people have traveled far to help your army destroy the Long Knives." He pointed to

Robert Dickson. "My brother and your countryman, Mascotapah, told us we would receive great rewards if we would come to your aid! Now you are telling us that we cannot take what will rightfully be ours?"

Captain Roberts replied firmly. "There will be many gifts seized from the American fort. You will share in all of these. Soon, when the war is over, there will be many more gifts granted to you by King George, your British father. You will get all of those, but if I am to honor the American commander's condition of truce, I must have your word that you will honor my pledge. You must swear to me that there will be no harm done to the fort or village, nor injury to its people. Your word must be your bond. Otherwise, I will not offer mine, and many of you will die."

An Ottawa chief shook his fists. "No!" he shouted. "We will take all that we see! It is the way!" He pointed at Dan, Kate and Pete. "You have let these Yankees sway your thoughts!"

Ojeeg and Leelinau rose quickly. They stood between their American friends and the others. "We have learned much from them," Ojeeg said. "They know of the times that will come."

A Wyandotte chief stared directly into Ojeeg's face. "How could they do that?" he asked angrily. "Many of our people, older and wiser than you, have been tricked by white man's words before."

"We can't tell you how they are able to see into the future," Leelinau said. "Only that it is true."

"You speak in this council as a Sioux and yet you are of mixed blood," another chief argued. "You should not even be here, let alone speak as an equal."

"We have been raised in the Indian ways," Leelinau

said, "but we have learned that not *all* Americans nor *all* British are our friends or our enemies—no more than all of our Indian brothers are friends or enemies to each other."

"It is true that my sister and I are *Metis*," Ojeeg added, "offspring of our white father and our Sioux mother. We know what it means to be outsiders. To our Sioux brothers we are thought of as white, and our white friends consider us Indian. These three Americans," he said, nodding toward Dan, Kate and Pete, "have told us that many years from now, people of this land will be as we are, a blend of many nations and colors. There will be no outcasts—only brothers and sisters in one great country—one that will stretch from where the sun rises to where it sets. Each will be judged, not on ancestry or color, but by integrity and merit."

"We know this Island is a sacred place to many of our Indian brothers," Leelinau said. "All of our nations have come here for generations and shared it in peace. Let this tradition continue. We must do as Captain Roberts asks. His words are wise. Let us accept the gifts he offers as our reward for helping our British friends."

Several moments passed as Captain Roberts surveyed the gathered leaders. "I must send a reply to Lieutenant Hanks," he said. "Any of you who are not with me, stand now and speak."

At that, there was much muttering, but none of the leaders rose.

Taking his quill in hand, Roberts signed the truce. "Mr. Dousman," Captain Roberts said, stepping away from the circle. "I would ask that you and your three friends join me at the fort."

Dousman turned to Dan, Kate and Pete. Dan and Kate

eagerly agreed. Pete, remembering his earlier walk across the battlefield in front of the American firing squad, shrugged. Finally, he nodded and followed the others to the fore.

Captain Roberts, along with two red-coated soldiers who played a slow, rhythmic tune on a fife and a drum, marched with the four Americans. The entourage moved down the hill and across the rifle range to Fort Michilimackinac. The gate opened to reveal, standing at attention on the parade grounds, the American commander and two officers.

"Lieutenant Hanks," Captain Roberts said, drawing the parchment from his coat pocket. "With the approval of the various leaders of my army, I have accepted your condition."

Hanks took the document and noted Captain Roberts' name at the bottom. He inked his quill and added his signature. "It is a decision that will benefit all parties," he said in relieved submission.

"Agreed," Captain Roberts said. "You and your men will lay down your arms and present yourselves as prisoners of war."

Lieutenant Hanks motioned for his soldiers to come from their positions along the north wall. They saluted Captain Roberts as they passed single file, each placing his rifle at the British officer's feet. Soon the entire American regiment had moved out through the north gate and into the hands of the British troops. Then the British fife and drum soldiers marched to the south sally port where the flagpole stood. At exactly noon, they brought down the American standard and raised, for the first time in sixteen years, the Union Jack over Fort Michilimackinac.

"Captain Roberts," Michael Dousman said, stepping

forward. "I know Moneypenny is eager to return to Fort St. Joseph's for a load of pelts. I would like to request that these three Americans be allowed passage to their homes, since the *Caledonia* will be passing their way."

"Indeed," Captain Roberts said. Then turning to Dan, Kate and Pete he added, "Because of your bravery, you have saved many lives." He reached into his pouch for his writing materials. He quickly jotted a note and handed it to Dousman. "Take this to Moneypenny. Though the message is brief, I believe it will ensure your friends a safe return. But you must hurry."

Dousman nodded, thinking of his time-traveling friends' final challenge. "I hope it will be that easy," he said.

"And why should it not?" Captain Roberts asked, looking puzzled.

"I doubt you'd believe me," the bearded Islander replied. "I'm not sure I understand it myself. We will find out soon, but first, we must go to the distillery. I have some explaining to do, and not everyone there will be happy to hear what I have to say."

The four Americans moved toward the fort's north gate. Meeting them there were Ojeeg and Leelinau.

"Our prophecy has been fulfilled," Leelinau said happily. "You really did come to us to bring peace to our people."

"It might only be for today," Pete said, "but at least a lot of people will live who would not have."

Kate stepped forward and embraced Leelinau. "If you and Ojeeg hadn't stood up at the council, it would not have happened."

Dan added, "I guess that's what your father had tried to tell you—that eventually you would find a way to use your heritage to advantage."

"Yes," Leelinau said, "for a moment I was worried that Red Thunder would not back down, but he is a good and reasonable chief. He saw the wisdom of our words."

"Now that your mission has been completed," Ojeeg said, "I'm sure you will return to your rightful time."

"I hope so," Dan said, looking concerned. Then, remembering Captain Roberts' warning about Moneypenny's departure, he added, "but now we must go."

"We will remember you always," Leelinau said.

The four Americans hurried down the hill to where Will and the rest of the villagers awaited under the watchful eye of the British guard.

CHAPTER 30
PETE MEETS A VERY IMPORTANT PERSON

As the four Americans approached the distillery, Dousman signaled to the British sentry. The guard opened the door, and Dan, Kate and Pete followed Dousman inside. Once there, Pete witnessed a scene of angry turmoil among the townspeople. Off to one side he saw Will standing with a very attractive girl, one who appeared vaguely familiar—but why, he could not guess.

Immediately, the boisterous crowd surrounded the four arrivals, grumbling loudly as they gathered.

"What's happening out there, Michael?" a man shouted.

Dousman raised his hand for silence. It was grudgingly given.

"As we told you when we met earlier at your homes," Dousman began, "a large British force has landed. It has advanced upon the fort and taken it. But rather than by force, it was done with a truce. England now controls the Island. As bad as that news is to many of you, at least you are safe. Your town will not be sacked. You can thank these four Americans for that," he said, gesturing toward Dan, Kate, Pete and Will.

"Explain yourself!" came an accusing voice. "How could four such young strangers have done *that*?"

"First, they helped me escape from the British ship's jail," Dousman said. "Then they convinced the British commander to let me take you to a place of safe refuge. Finally, and most importantly, they devised a plan that would persuade Captain Roberts that, rather than engage in battle, he should strike a deal with

Lieutenant Hanks."

"What kind of deal?" a woman in the back pressed.

"In exchange for turning over the fort, Hanks made Captain Roberts pledge there would be no damage to the village and that the people would be left unharmed."

"If that was agreed, what did Roberts get in return?" a man snapped.

There was much shouting from the American people. Dousman raised his hand for silence. "No more than what a victorious army would have expected—and perhaps a lot less," he replied. He waited a moment for the grumbling to subside. "Each of us must take an oath of allegiance to the Crown or leave the Island," he reported.

Loud shouts again rose from the Americans. "So, we kneel to the King or lose our property?" a man yelled. "What kind of a deal is that?"

"It is one we can live with," Dousman replied calmly.

"I will never again suffer under British rule," a woman shouted. "I watched those tyrants torture and murder my parents."

"What's to become of my children . . . and my *shop*?" the village harness maker added.

"All property will remain in the hands of its owners," Dousman said. "If you do not sign the oath of allegiance, you must leave. Still, you will have a month to get your affairs in order. Under the circumstances, Captain Roberts has made a most generous offer. The Indians and Frenchmen have pledged that they will do no harm to you or your possessions—a consent not easily gained, as I, myself, witnessed."

"I'll believe *that* tomorrow morning when I wake up and my home is still standing," hollered a man cynically.

"Aye, and my children's scalps remain on their heads!" another cried.

At that, shouts rang out around the hall. Men and women pushed and shoved one another in frustration and resentment.

"We should have come to the fort and fought along with our soldiers," an irate man fumed.

Dousman stood calmly at the front of the crowd and again raised his hand for silence. Slowly, the Islanders quieted. "Any gunfire from the fort would have led to certain massacre," he said flatly. "We would all have died—a result that would have served no one—British, American, French, Irish or Indian. I'm of the mind that we pick our battles—and live to fight another day. A dead patriot can do no more for his country. In time, we will rise from this and regain our place—but we will do it peacefully."

Dousman stepped to a window and peered across Mackinac Harbor. "It looks to be safe for us to return to our homes," he announced. He nodded to the British soldier, who stepped outside and held the opened door. In the distance, all could hear the victors' shouts of celebration. The British soldiers fired cannon, rifles and, in general, reacted joyously but peaceably to their victory.

As the Islanders filed past Mr. Dousman, some thanked him for his efforts, while others vented anger. Mackinac would remain an island divided in allegiance—perhaps forever.

When all the villagers had left the distillery, only six people remained inside—Dan, Kate, Pete, Mr. Dousman, Will Drake and his new friend, the girl he had met that morning.

"We haven't been introduced," Kate said, facing the

Island girl.

"I'm sorry," Will said. He took the girl's hand in his. "Averill, this is Dan, Kate and Pete. And you must know Mr. Dousman. Everyone, I would like you to meet Averill Newcastle. She is the daughter of the village blacksmith. Her mother, father and brother came here from England ten years ago."

At the mention of Averill's name, Pete stared at her—his jaw open. It was as if a cannonball had struck him dumb. He stared for a moment. He then blinked in a sudden flash of understanding. He remembered his mother telling him that Will Drake had come to Mackinac and met an Island girl. They were married and lived long and rewarding lives. *She* was the missing piece of the puzzle.

Kate glanced quizzically at Pete and then faced Will and Averill. "The rest of us had better get back to the boat," she said. "Captain Roberts told us that we could return to the Snows aboard the *Caledonia*. I hope she hasn't already left."

"I had better go with you to the ship," Dousman said. "We will take the longboat and row back now."

Seeing Will Drake holding Averill's hand, Pete asked, "Will, are you coming with us?"

"No, Pete," Will said, shaking his head. "My journey is over. I am home. As you must know, my future is here. I have every reason to stay. You, more so than anyone, must understand that I cannot go where you hope to return."

Pete nodded, understanding Will's riddle. "I will remember you for as long as I live," Pete said, a lump forming in this throat. He stepped toward his ancestor. The two held each other closely, not as young men might do to congratulate each other following a sporting event, but more as a parent and child when they know their parting will be forever.

"And I, you," Will replied. "Now I must bid you farewell and Godspeed." He released his embrace with Pete and grasped Averill's hand. She took Will's arm in hers.

Pete rubbed his eyes as he glanced from Will to Averill. He saw in her smile the reason she had reminded him of someone else. She looked just like the picture of his mom in her high school yearbook.

In the distance, Pete saw Dan and Kate hurrying with Dousman along the shore toward the rowboat. Kate turned and called urgently, "Pete, we're going!"

Pete gave Will and Averill one more look and then ran to the beach. The bearded Islander once again sat in the boat's stern, and the others took their positions on the thwarts. Soon they were rowing back to the northwest end of the Island. There, at British Landing, they found the *Caledonia* tugging gently at her anchor.

As the rowboat neared the tall ship, Pete turned to see, scrambling among the crosstrees, a dozen men, setting the sails. On the main deck, six British soldiers stood awaiting the return to their old fort.

Pete scanned the ship for one person in particular. Standing near the helm next to Moneypenny was Skaggs. His face was a brilliant crimson, a picture of rage as he stared down at the rowboat.

"There you are!" he shouted. "I'll make you regret what you did to me if it's the last thing I do!"

Ignoring the British soldier's warning, Dousman called to Moneypenny. "Permission to board?" he asked. "I bear orders from Captain Roberts."

"Permission granted," Moneypenny answered. "Heave to and tie off."

215

At that, Dousman called for two more strokes from his rowing crew. The longboat drew alongside the *Caledonia* just as a rope ladder was dropped from the ship. Pete tied the rowboat to it and then pulled himself up to the deck. Kate, Dan and Dousman quickly followed. Once aboard, Dousman handed Mr. Moneypenny the note Captain Roberts had given him. Moneypenny opened it and read aloud:

17 July, 1812
To Captain Moneypenny,

Please be advised that the American conscripts who were pressed into service three days ago must be returned safely to the Les Cheneaux Islands where you mistook them for enemy sailors. Do this with all speed, for I regret this error has inconvenienced them greatly. Their misfortune has, however, led to the saving of many of our troops and most, if not all, of the people of Mackinac Island, soldiers and civilians alike. Their service to both countries has been invaluable. They must be treated with utmost regard and granted full marks for courage, valor and citizenship. Your attention to this matter will be noted in my correspondence to General Brock as well as His Majesty, King George III.

Respectfully,

Captain Charles Roberts

"I believe *that* should ensure the Americans a timely return to their place of capture," Dousman said.

"Indeed it shall," Moneypenny replied. He turned to the young Americans. "We will be casting off shortly," he said. "You may return to your quarters and gather your belongings. I believe you know the way. Change into your own clothes and settle your account with Mr. Farnsworth. I'll send word to expect you."

As Pete led the others along the deck, Arnold Skaggs stepped ahead and blocked their way.

"Sergeant Skaggs," Moneypenny said calmly. "These people are no longer your prisoners. You may remain with me on deck. Don't make me wish I didn't agree to take you back to General Brock."

Skaggs froze, his eyes on Pete.

"Excuse us," Pete said pleasantly, stepping around the fuming soldier. The veins in Skaggs' neck nearly exploded as the three Americans moved around him.

"Did you hear that?" Dan said, following Pete. "We can get our own clothes and dump these outfits."

"I didn't like them from the first time I heard them called 'slops,'" Kate said with a laugh.

"Give me my cutoffs and T-shirt any day," Dan said.

Pete glanced at his uniform. "I kind of like it," he said with a shrug. "Besides, this is all I came with."

They went directly to their room and found their old clothes where they'd left them under the tattered sail. Kate took her yellow jacket from the floor where Skaggs had thrown it after a *Caledonia* sailor had found him and untied him. The jacket appeared none the worse for the wear it had seen. The boys stayed outside as Kate changed into her original pirate outfit. Dan followed. Shortly, all three had gathered their hammocks and were on their way to the ship's store.

There, Mr. Farnsworth sat, his eyes beaming in delight. Word had passed quickly from the quarterdeck that his three American customers were now to be treated as honored guests.

"So, I suppose yeh'll be wanting a full refund, will yeh now," he said with a knowing grin.

Dan and Kate nodded as they held out their uniforms and hammocks to the one-armed man.

"Boots and hose, as well," Farnsworth reminded them. "Got it right here," he said, pointing to his gilt-edged book. Dan and Kate took off their shoes and socks and handed them to the storekeeper. The man turned to the entry of July 14th, inked his quill and marked *Rtd* next to the twins' purchases.

At that, Pete stepped forward and handed his shoes and stockings to the man. "I'd like my penny back," he said.

Mr. Farnsworth chuckled. "Saw yeh climb the mast, I did. Yeh got more'n a penny's worth o' use out o' *that,* sure enough. But then, so did we all. Ship might a' gone down if yeh hadn't done what yeh done." He chortled again as he reached into the cash box. He searched around for a moment and pulled out the same black coin Pete had given him three days before. "Ah, yes, this is it. Now maybe you can tell me why this here penny, minted in London only last year, could have gotten so tarnished in such a short time. Looks to be a hunnert years old, sure it does."

"Yeah, you're right," Pete answered. "Maybe more, but that's how it was when I found it."

"Umm, mighty strange," Farnsworth said, studying Pete suspiciously. He flipped the coin to Pete and then scrawled *Rfnd* next to his name. "You are excused," he said, dismissing the three with a wave.

Dan led the others out the storeroom door and up the companionway stairs.

Kate stared quizzically at Pete. "Say, Pete," she said, "I saw the look on your face when Will introduced us to Averill. I thought you were going to pass out right there. What was *that* all about?"

"*She* is why we came," Pete said simply. He then smiled and added, "Averill and Will are going to get married one day—and you're looking at the grand result of it all."

"What do you mean?" Kate asked.

"The name 'Averill' has been in our family for years—it's my mom's, for one," Pete said. "I asked her once where it came from. She told me it was for her great-great-grandmother. Every generation afterward, the first daughter was called Averill. It dawned on me as Will introduced her to us that I was standing with my ancestors on the day they met. And it was not for *Will* we had come so far to help, but for *Averill*, this Island girl, who would otherwise not have survived the day! It became clear why all three of us had been needed for this job. We each are good at different things, and with all of us working together we saved, not only Will's life, but Averill's as well. Plus, we made sure they met. That's why I'm sure we're going home—to our real home."

"Well, we're not there yet," Dan pointed out. "And I honestly don't know how, by simply sailing back to the Snows, that is going to change. What are we going to do if we get back to Gravelly Island and it's still 1812?"

"I think Ojeeg and Leelinau had it right," Pete said. "According to their legend, people return to their own time after they've done what they came to do."

"I sure hope you're right," Dan said.

"Me, too," Kate said. "We're not out of the woods yet."

The three Americans reached the main deck and went up the stairs to the ship's helm. The *Caledonia* had not, as yet, cast off. Skaggs, still seething with rage, stood at Moneypenny's side. Dousman, too, was there.

The ship's captain turned to his former prisoners as they approached. "I shouldn't ask for help from such important people as yourselves," he said smiling, "but would you be willing to assist with the anchor?"

"You bet," Pete said at once. "Anything to get back home."

"I have to return to the village," Dousman said to Moneypenny. He turned to his American friends. "Farewell. I hope you make it *all* the way home," he said with a wink. "If you don't and you need my help, you'll know where to find me." He stepped down the boarding ladder to the rowboat. "Godspeed," he called as he waved.

"Man your stations!" Moneypenny called to his crew. "Prepare to hoist anchor!"

The three Americans went to the capstan and formed a circle around the barrel. Three other sailors jumped to their sides. The bosun started a hearty chant. "It's round Cape Horn we're off to go . . ."

" . . . Go down, ye blood-red roses, go down," Pete, Dan and Kate sang, lifting their voices even more loudly than the chanteyman himself.

In minutes, the anchor was weighed and the merchant ship had cleared British Landing. A good breeze at the *Caledonia*'s stern sent her smartly toward the Les Cheneaux Islands. The three friends went up to the quarterdeck, where they stood with Mr. Moneypenny. They gazed intently into the distance as the ship sailed east.

In three hours' time they passed Goose Island, where Michael Dousman had been taken captive the night before.

Just ahead, Pete saw Marquette Island, the largest and most westerly in the Les Cheneaux chain. He stared intently, hoping to see a cottage—a motorboat—anything modern in the distance. He did not.

The *Caledonia* sailed on. Where Hessel Village should have been, only a dense forest could be seen. Pete was losing his confidence as it appeared that Dan's and Kate's fears might come true. The tall ship cruised past Little LaSalle, Big LaSalle, Government and Boot Islands. No trace could they see of the lively resort community they had left three days ago.

As they approached Gravelly Island, the smallest and least likely to have any evidence of civilization, a thin line of smoke appeared near the island's southern tip.

"Look!" Pete said excitedly. "Is that a campfire?"

"Looks like it," Dan said flatly, "but it's probably just a tribe of Indians on their way home from Mackinac."

"Maybe it's the Sioux," Kate said. "It could be Leelinau and Ojeeg. They had a couple hours' head start on us."

Pete glanced away from the trail of smoke. Something caught his eye. He raced to Moneypenny. "May I borrow your spyglass?" he asked.

"Certainly," the captain replied, handing Pete the brass instrument. "What do you see?"

"Not sure," Pete said, adjusting the glass. A split second later he shouted, "There!" he said, pointing to a small dot on the horizon. "Take us there!" He returned the spyglass to the captain.

Moneypenny extended the device to its full length.

221

He turned to his first mate and called, "Ahoy! All hands on deck! Make ready to change course!"

CHAPTER 31
FAREWELL AND HELLO

Kate and Dan jumped to the captain's side, each grabbing frantically for the spyglass.

There was much scurrying about as Moneypenny called orders to his sailors, bringing the *Caledonia* toward the tiny dot on the horizon. Soon, all aboard could see the canoe-shaped vessel, straining at its anchor and bobbing with the long Lake Huron swells. Presently, the tall ship hove to, her port side nudging the *Captain Bing*.

"Drop the ladder," the skipper called. At that, a British sailor tossed the landing rope down to the craft. Moneypenny glanced at his three American charges. "You would choose this useless dinghy to a three-masted schooner?" he asked in disbelief.

"Yes, sir," Pete said. "We hope it will take us home."

"I will leave you here then, if that is your wish," Moneypenny said, shaking his head, "but I don't see how you'll get it to shore."

"We'll take our chances," Kate said excitedly, her eye on the boat below. She was first to go over the rail and down the ladder. Dan was right behind. The two were soon anxiously looking up at Pete who remained with the captain. If the two boats became separated by a sudden gust of wind, Pete could be trapped aboard the tall ship and lost in the past forever.

"Come on!" Kate called.

Pete offered his right hand to Mr. Moneypenny. "Thanks for bringing us back," he said.

"I'm really sorry to see you leave," the captain

replied, accepting Pete's grip. "Something very strange has been going on these past few days, and I'd really like an explanation."

Pete answered, "So would I," with a wry grin.

Just then, Skaggs came scurrying up from behind, looking wilder than a wet weasel. "You're not going to get away that easy," he yelled angrily. "I owe you this!"

Pete turned just in time to see the red-faced soldier uncork a haymaker aimed for his left ear. He ducked and Skaggs' blow whistled over his head. Mr. Moneypenny reached up and caught the soldier's fist in his own left hand.

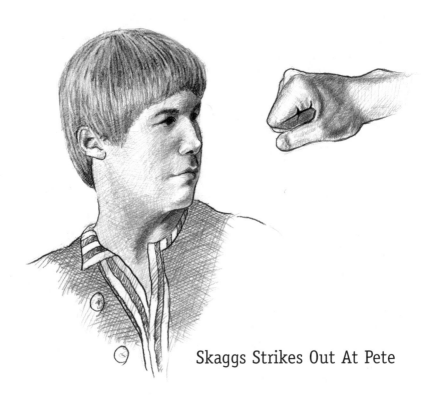

Skaggs Strikes Out At Pete

"That bit of insubordination will land you in the brig for the duration of our journey," the captain said calmly. "Having you back in the hands of General Brock will be the happiest day of my life. I believe my American friends had it right when they tied you to that cell door."

"I guess I'd better go," Pete said. "My friends are waiting." He then disappeared over the side, hurried down the ladder and went to the *Bing*'s stern.

"Farewell," Moneypenny called with a wave. He then turned to his crew and ordered, "Trim sail cheerily, gentlemen!" At that, the *Caledonia*'s sailors leapt to their posts.

As Pete stood at the *Bing*'s helm, Dan turned to him and said, "All right, Pete, crank 'er up. It'll probably take a few pulls to get 'er going . . . as long as it's been."

Pete reached down and took hold of the handle. He pulled it and, surprisingly, the *Bing* responded immediately with a low-pitched chug . . chug . . chug. Pete glanced at Dan and Kate, who gazed at the motor with a look of surprise.

"Go figure," Dan said with a shrug. "You must have the touch. Even Mr. Heuck never gets her started on the first pull."

Pete left the gear in neutral as Dan and Kate brought in yard after yard of anchor line. As they did, the *Bing* drifted farther away from Gravelly Island. Finally, as the twins stowed the hook safely in the bow, Pete became aware of a warm, almost hot breeze coming from the west. He glanced toward Gravelly Island and the strand of white smoke. He turned again to check the position of the *Caledonia*. It wasn't there! He spun completely around, scanning the entire horizon. The tall ship had vanished! As suddenly as it had appeared three days ago, it was now nowhere to be seen.

"Where should we go?" Kate asked, peeling off her yellow jacket.

"I'd say Gravelly Island," Pete answered.

"What if the smoke *is* from an Indian fire?" Dan asked. "It could be one of the tribes we met at Mackinac. Some of them weren't very happy with us. Maybe we should go the other way and see what's on Island Number Eight."

"That fire is the only sign of life in any direction," Pete differed. "I say we head there."

"I guess there's no sense going anywhere else," Kate agreed. "My vote's with Gravelly, too."

"Aye, aye," Pete said. He pushed the gear forward and turned the wheel, aiming the bow toward the slim trail of smoke.

As the *Bing* neared the island, Pete could see figures moving along the beach. As the boat drew closer, he realized they were dressed in bright colors. "Their clothes sure don't look anything like what the Indians were wearing at Mackinac," he said.

"Right," Dan agreed. "But it can't be our crowd. Mr. Heuck would have taken them home three days ago."

"Maybe it's a search party," Kate guessed. "I bet every policeman in the U.P. is looking for us."

"If it *is* a search party, what will we tell them?" Dan asked. "How do we explain where we've been for so long?"

"We'll just tell them the truth," Pete said. "We got snatched up by some British sailors who took us back to 1812."

"Oh, yeah," Dan scoffed, "and who would believe *that*?"

"Yeah, good point," Pete agreed. "Okay, maybe we could tell them the *Bing* conked out or something. It took us three days, but we just now got her going."

The closer Pete brought the boat to shore, the more it seemed that the people *were* wearing modern clothes. "I really think we're back!" Kate shouted.

Dan yipped in agreement. "We made it!"he cheered.

The *Bing* was now close enough for Pete to see people's faces. "That's Neal Preston!" he shouted. "I'd know his white hair anywhere!"

"You're right, Pete!" Dan exclaimed. "And that's Mr. Heuck standing by the fire! They all must be part of the search team."

Pete kept the *Bing* pointed straight for shore. The closer he got, the more people he recognized boys— Trip, Duke and Moose, and girls—Jane, Nancy and Stella. Soon all three of the *Bing*'s crew were yelling at the tops of their lungs. "Ahoy! Ahoy!" they cheered. Pete had never been so happy to see familiar faces in his life!

A few of the party casually turned and watched the *Bing* approach, but most simply went on with what they were doing. Some gathered wood. Some set plates on a makeshift table. Some just stood in small groups, chatting among themselves. None seemed terribly excited to see their long lost friends.

"They must be pretty mad at us," Kate said.

The *Bing* was almost to shore when Mr. Heuck cupped his hands to his mouth and called, "What are you doing? It's been fifteen minutes! Aren't you going to anchor off?"

At once, Pete, Dan and Kate's jaws dropped. They stood dumbstruck as the *Bing* coasted up to the beach. Pete almost rammed the island before cutting the

227

engine. The boat slowed, then ground to a halt, nearly launching its passengers over the bow. Dan and Kate scrambled to their feet and stared at Mr. Heuck. Pete cast his gaze upon the other people. Nobody even moved to greet them. Their indifference was bewildering. Kate leaped from the bow onto the island and was quickly followed by her brother.

"Fifteen minutes?" Kate asked, eyeing Mr. Heuck suspiciously.

Neal Preston approached, holding an armful of kindling. "Yeah, what were you doing?" he asked, accusingly. "You were supposed to anchor the *Bing*, not take her on a joy ride. Thirty yards offshore is what Mr. Heuck said. I heard him! You took her out a mile! Then, when you *did* drop anchor, it no sooner hit bottom than you brought it up. What was *that* all about?"

Dan stared again at Mr. Heuck. He glanced from face to face, expecting to see someone crack a smile. "You're kidding, right?" he muttered. "Another joke?"

Mr. Heuck noticed Dan's puzzled expression. "What do you mean?" he asked softly.

"None of you saw a rather large old sailboat out there?" Dan asked, searching his friends' eyes. "A three-masted, 19th-century schooner?"

Neal pushed himself in front of Dan. "No! And neither did you," he scoffed. "If you're trying to get out of helping, well, it won't work. The fire is going, but there's still lots to do."

Pete suddenly realized the entire truth. He and his two friends had somehow spent the past three days in 1812, but in real time the entire adventure had happened in the blink of an eye. If that were true, then how could they ever convince the others about the *Caledonia*, Leelinau and Ojeeg, Mascotapah, St. Joseph's

Island, Michael Dousman, the fort, the pine tree, Will Drake, Averill Newcastle—any of that—without trying to prove that it had all happened in practically no time at all? He looked into the questioning eyes of Mr. Heuck and the rest of the Pirate Party as they awaited an answer.

"So," Neal taunted, "are you going to tell us what you were doing, or are you just going to stand there, gawking like a bunch of idiots?"

Pete turned to Neal and then the others. "For being gone only fifteen minutes, it's kind of a long story," he said. "For one thing, Dan and Kate saved my life." He glanced at the twins, who by their expressions, showed that they also understood what had happened and the futility of trying to explain it to the others.

-     -   -   -   -

The rest of the day went pretty much as Mr. Heuck had planned. Over the next few hours, the pirates discovered all his hidden clues and followed them to wonderful trinkets scattered from one end of Treasure Island to the other. There was plenty of loot for everyone. Oh, aye, it was a grand and glorious day, sure it was, and all the privateers, including Pirate Pete, Dangerous Dan and Cantankerous Kate enjoyed the last afternoon to its fullest.

Towards the end, however, Dan, Kate and Pete seemed a little more tired than the rest, and not quite as interested in the pirate talk as the others.

Shadows began to lengthen over Gravelly Island, and a crisp, cool breeze swept through the Snows. By six o'clock, or four bells, as Mr. Heuck reckoned, he directed all his buccaneers to tidy the beach, douse the campfire and board the *Captain Bing*.

Soon, the small gray vessel was chugging through the marvelously blue Lake Huron water, the Les Cheneaux Islands coming and passing on either side. Pete, Dan and Kate were sitting quietly with Mr. Heuck in the stern.

"One thing I've got to ask," Dan said to Pete. "How did *Caledonia*'s account book get under the floor boards at Fort Mackinac?"

"Right," Kate said. "How did it get from the supply room of a British ship to the officers' quarters of an American fort?"

Pete pulled the ledger from his jacket pocket. "I don't know," he said. "But there's something else about this that's been bugging me."

What's that?" Kate asked.

Pete looked up from the book and stared first at Kate and then Dan. "Why did this get hot but my sailor's uniform and the British penny stay normal? If it was like we thought, you know, the book changed temperature because its double was so close, well then, the same thing should have happened to my clothes and the coin. But they didn't."

Dan picked up the ledger and thumbed through its pages. "That's right. Do you suppose this is how we got where we did—back to 1812, I mean? This book—could it be like a door or something?"

"Wow!" Kate whispered. "I'll bet you're right. Pete and I had just been reading the entry for July 14th 1812 when the *Caledonia* came along. Maybe we can go to any place and any time that's mentioned in that book!"

"That's seems a bit far-fetched," Pete scoffed.

"No more than what we've just been through," Kate said. "What if it's true and we really can go back in time to whatever's written in that book?"

"That'd be pretty wild," Dan said. "We could find out anything in history we'd ever want to know."

"As long as it's in Pete's book," Kate reminded him.

"Right," Dan said. "What I'd first like to do is find out more about the *Caledonia*. That was one cool ship. I wonder what it did for the rest of the war."

"And I wonder what became of Mr. Dousman—and all the others," Kate added.

"Mr. Porter called it the 'Forgotten War,'" Pete said. "But *I* won't forget it any time soon."

"I suppose," Dan said with a laugh, "that we can now tell Mr. Porter the names of those people in the truce party—the ones he said were lost to history—us, as it turns out."

"Think we should?" Pete asked.

"Think he'd believe us?" Kate answered wryly.

-     -   -   -   -

For the rest of the way home, the three friends barely spoke—even to each other. Instead, each stared at the shoreline and stored memories of the past three days.

An hour later, Mr. Heuck guided the *Bing* to its mooring place inside his boathouse. His pirates gathered their treasures and set off to their cottages throughout the Snows. Pete walked with Dan and Kate to their place on Cincinnati Row and then waved goodbye. He continued through the darkening trail along the shore to his own cabin in Elliot Bay.

-     -   -   -   -

That evening, Pete folded Will Drake's pirate clothes and set them into the bottom of the old cedar chest. As he held the jacket, he came across the mysterious book and the large British penny. He flipped the coin once and started to slip it into his jeans pocket.

What a great souvenir, he thought. He'd be able to show it to his friends back home and tell them all about his amazing summer adventure.

Then he stopped. They'd never believe him. Instead, he tucked it back into the vest pocket with the accounts book. After all, it wasn't *his* to keep. He'd only borrowed it from his friend—his 'friend' being his own great-great-great-grandfather. Besides, the next person to wear the jacket might just meet a certain 19th-century, three-masted schooner and need a penny for some socks and shoes.

CHAPTER 32
EPILOGUE

The year is 2012. The date: August 27. The place: an immense boathouse along Cincinnati Row in the Les Cheneaux Islands of Michigan's upper peninsula.

There is much hustle and bustle this morning as a large canoe-shaped vessel, festooned from stem to stern with small, colorful pennants and one large Jolly Roger flag, backs from its mooring place into Cedarville Channel. Twenty young people aboard are chatting, laughing and carrying on excitedly. Several, standing in the bow, are belting out, "Sixteen men on a dead man's chest." Others are talking boisterously in a dialect that could only be described as Pirate-ese. The strange boat turns toward open water and begins its voyage for an uncharted Treasure Island.

At the ship's helm stands a slim, suntanned, ever-youthful man. His age? That's hard to say—a good guess would be somewhere between forty and eighty. He has always been and will ever be a kid at heart. He towers over most of his crew—children as young as six— but by some of the teens, he is dwarfed. Certainly by all he is loved as their very own Captain Heuck. He sports an eye patch, a goatee and an outrageously wild pirate outfit. In fact, all aboard the Bing are attired in buccaneer garb.

One such privateer seems to be wearing genuinely antique clothes. The attractive sailor is clad in white knickers, a black hat, black shoes and a red-and-white-striped shirt. This young pirate approaches the captain with a smile while holding a gilt-edged book and a large, black coin found only moments ago tucked snugly in her vest pocket.

POSTSCRIPT

<u>In the story, what is real and what is made up</u>?

The <u>Cincinnati Row kids</u> are real, but I've changed their names—somewhat. Pete Jenkins (me) is real, but Pete did, in one summer, more than I did in a dozen. Pete's parents and sister are real, and Will Drake was a real person, but the character he portrays is not.

<u>Robert Dickson</u> and <u>Chief Red Thunder</u> are real and did take part in the attack as in the story, but <u>Ojeeg</u> and <u>Leelinau</u> are names that I took from Henry Schoolcraft's *Indian Legends*. Their names and meanings are real, but the characters they portray are imaginary. Their place in the story is to make a link to other historic events, which are real. Their moods and attitudes might be that of people like them at that time.

The names <u>Moneypenny</u> and <u>Skaggs</u> are fictitious, but a man whom I chose to call Mr. Moneypenny did captain the *Caledonia* for the British-owned North West Fur Company and brought orders from General Isaac Brock to Captain Charles Roberts at Fort St. Joseph's in the St. Mary's River. Brock very likely sent a soldier, someone like Skaggs but whose real name is lost in antiquity, to complete that mission for the British general.

Lieutenant Porter Hanks, Michael Dousman, Robert Dickson, and Captain Charles Roberts all did in real life what was related in the story.

What became of them?

After the capture of Fort Mackinac, Lieutenant Porter Hanks and the other American soldiers were ordered by Captain Roberts to board two captured American vessels, the *Mary* and the *Selina*. On July 26, 1812, they were taken to Fort Detroit which, for the moment, was still in U.S. hands. By the gentlemanly rules of war at that time, they were sworn to remain out of active service to their country and not take up arms against the British. On August 16, a month after the attack, Porter Hanks was in a Fort Detroit courtroom being questioned about the surrender at Michilimackinac. While he was sitting on the stand, a British cannonball, shot from Windsor across the Detroit River, tore through the wall and struck him dead. Later that day, General William Hull, in a highly controversial decision, surrendered Fort Detroit to the enemy.

Michael Dousman enjoyed a long, productive and interesting life. A shrewd politician and an astute businessman, Mr. Dousman's efforts to protect the Mackinac Island citizens, however, were not without detractors. Some Islanders regarded his acts as totally self-serving or even worse, treasonous. Such people accused him of selling out to the British. As evidence, they pointed to the fact that the new British commander of the fort, Charles Roberts, allowed Dousman to remain on Mackinac Island without forcing him to declare allegiance to the Crown as was required of the other American sympathizers. Dousman also was allowed to travel freely within British areas and continued his fur-trading activities. He also acquired—

by, to some, questionable means—several tracts of land both on and off Mackinac Island.

On the other hand, to Michael Dousman's credit, he *did* save the lives of every Mackinac Islander, military and civilian, from certain massacre. Also, he was a family man with a wife, a daughter and a son. His actions on the night and morning of July 16 and 17, 1812, did indeed change the course of Mackinac Island history.

Michael Dousman's business accomplishments included his fur-trading ventures, his farm on the Island and ownership of a lumber mill (Mill Creek) south of Mackinaw City. Also, he must have been highly regarded by the community because he was elected president of the Mackinac Island Village Council in 1824-25 and probate judge from 1833-40. He died a wealthy man on August 24, 1854.

Robert Dickson, *Mascotapah* to his Native American friends, lived in real life the events depicted in the story. It's hard to characterize any modern-day person as a pioneer, explorer or adventurer in the same way as Robert Dickson was during the early 1800s. He set sail as a young man from Scotland to the New World to become a fur trader and take on all the uncertainties of this uncharted and wild continent. To do that successfully, he had to become an interpreter of the Native American languages, deal faithfully with its varied indigenous peoples and become a trusted agent for all parties concerned. It was a dangerous venture, but an exciting one. Mackinac Island was his first camp. It was there that he met a beautiful Indian princess, To-to-win, sister of Red Thunder, chief of a Sioux tribe. They fell instantly in love and married.

Because of their relationship, he met many tribesmen and acted as translator while pursuing his duties for the

North West Fur Company. After the British attack at Mackinac Island, he became an active participant in the community, helping Captain Roberts and subsequent commanders maintain control at the fort until the United States regained it in 1815. In this story, I have touched only briefly on the life of one of North America's most interesting frontiersmen.

<u>Captain Charles Roberts</u> was, in fact, the commander of Fort St. Joseph's and did attack Mackinac Island as told in the story. By 1812 he had served his country's army at camps all over the British Empire and had suffered his share of hard conditions and dangerous duties. At the tiny outpost on St. Mary's Island, he was in charge of a small garrison of worn-out old soldiers, the Tenth Royal Veteran Battalion. In addition to his ineffective garrison of retirees was a conglomeration of recruits—a hundred Canadian woodsmen and nearly a thousand Native Americans—gathered to attack the much more strategic location of Fort Michilimackinac, held by the United States. To give you an idea of the resulting situation, I offer this direct quote from Captain Roberts while his combined troops were encamped at Fort St. Joseph's in the days leading up to the attack:

"Although it is quite impossible to make my French and Indian allies do even the simplest drills, they each have the strength and will of ten of my regular soldiers. The French train, if you can call it that, with a pipe in their mouths and their daily rations of pork and bread skewered on their bayonets. When they are called to drill in formation they simply laugh."

After taking command of Fort Mackinac in 1812, Captain Roberts suffered through a brutally cold winter in the Straits. His entire garrison was forced into near starvation, reduced to eating their horses to survive until spring. Already in fragile health from years of service to the British army, Captain Roberts' condition weakened as a result of that terrible season. When the ice broke in the spring of 1813, he sent word to General Provost, requesting relief from his duties, but that was not granted until that September. He died in 1817 in Canada, having never fully recovered from the accumulated effects of his ailments.

John Jacob Astor never visited Mackinac Island, but his influence was enormous. He was the undisputed king of the fur trade that may have been the ultimate reason for the War of 1812. It is hard for us to imagine in our present-day lives in a time when oil production controls the world economy, that there was a period when animal furs did the same thing. Just as fossil fuels now keep us warm, processed pelts from wild animals did the same two hundred years ago. The fur-bearing animals in the highly populated areas of Asia and Europe had been hunted almost to extinction. Millions of people there were desperate for warm clothing. The Chinese produced lots of tea, which the British loved with a passion and could not get anywhere else. Mr. Astor, a recent German immigrant to the United States, sold his pelts in the Orient for huge quantities of tea leaves, which he sold in England. With some of the profits, he brought British trade goods to the United States. Those goods, in turn, were used to trade with the Indians for more pelts. With every transaction Mr. Astor made a handsome profit that made him the wealthiest American of his day.

What was the war all about?
The Treaty of Paris in 1783, which officially ended the American War of Independence, or the

Revolutionary War as we now call it, left a lot of loose ends. The British negotiators back in England unexpectedly ceded to the Americans the Northwest Territory, a huge tract of land that now includes Ohio, Indiana, Illinois, Michigan, Wisconsin and part of Minnesota. The British owners of the North West Fur Company were angry that their government had given up this valuable land to the Americans. So, instead of quitting their lucrative fur dealings, they simply retained their forts at Detroit, Michilimackinac and Niagara and continued to trade with the Indians as though nothing had changed. Also, Indian tribes, who at this point favored the British over the American agents, continued working with the British traders.

It wasn't until U.S. General Anthony Wayne defeated the Indians at Fallen Timbers in Ohio in 1794 that the British government gave over the frontier forts to the United States in 1797. Still, the British fur traders did not give up their fur-trading activities. Nor did their Indian allies.

After Fallen Timbers, the Indians slowly gave over small portions of land to the Americans in treaties. Then, in 1809, the great Shawnee chief Tecumseh attempted to gather all the various tribes together. He preached to his people that they should cast aside the evils of the white man's ways. If they united themselves, they could keep what land they still controlled and live happily by their old customs. In spite of Tecumseh's promise to the U.S. government that his confederacy of tribes was strictly a defensive measure, William Henry Harrison, then governor of Indiana Territory, suspected a major Indian rebellion.

Harrison feared the American settlers would be massacred by Tecumseh's followers, leaving villages burned and settlers' hopes for further westward migration dashed in the Indians' wake. So, in November of 1811, Harrison, with a large army, marched up the Wabash River to Tecumseh's brother's camp at the mouth of the Tippecanoe River and defeated the collected Indian tribes in a long and deadly battle. Reports following that conflict made Americans believe that the British government had supplied the Indians with guns used in their defense, and it was the scheming British who had contrived to support the Indian confederacy. Tempers between British and American combatants grew short. Each suspected that the other was about to attack.

Some American leaders such as Henry Clay and John Calhoun, known as War Hawks, felt it was time to drive the British out of this continent once and for all. Once the British were gone, they felt the Indians would also cave and the future American settlers would be safe. With the Frenchman Napoleon Bonaparte advancing steadily toward a conflict on English soil, the War Hawks believed that was the time to start such a campaign. Soon the British army would leave the American continent to concentrate their energies on the real threat to their homeland.

Also, back in England, Parliament was certain the fledgling Colonies' government would soon collapse under its own weight. The new country would surely come crawling back to its homeland for leadership. Democracy, a largely unproven form of government on such a large scale, was bound to fail. Evidence of this notion existed in abundance. Incessant bickering between the northern and southern states over slavery, economy and ideology would conquer them without any intervention from the British military. It was just a matter of time.

But as the years went by and the United States *didn't*

collapse as quickly as Parliament had predicted, British military leaders decided to set up a blockade to keep American businesses from selling supplies to Britain's primary enemy, France. When the blockade didn't work quickly enough, the British Navy began to stop American vessels on the open sea. They searched its ships and captured the American sailors, forcing them to serve aboard the British merchant frigates. Their excuse was that American sailors were nothing more than traitors to the Crown and were to be treated as British prisoners.

As a result of this blockade, American businessmen suffered and the struggling nation's economy got worse. Finally, by the spring of 1812, most of our seaport merchants were nearly bankrupt. On June 18, 1812, James Madison asked Congress to declare war. Once passed, word of the conflict was slow to reach the people in the outlying areas, often not being known until months later. The message did not arrive at Fort Michilimackinac until 10 a.m., July 17,1812. It was delivered to Lieutenant Hanks by a group of Mackinac Islanders sent under a flag of truce by Captain Charles Roberts of the British Army, much as described in the story.

Just as America had Henry Clay and John Calhoun, its War Hawks, the British had their own leaders who were eager to reclaim the continent for their King. George Prevost, John Simcoe and Captain Gray had aims of making the United States return *all* its land to Britain.

General Isaac Brock led the British forces in Upper Canada. He recognized the strategic importance of Michilimackinac. For over six months before the war was declared, Brock had planned that Captain Roberts' garrison at Fort St. Joseph's, with the help of as many

Indian and Canadian woodsmen as he could get, would launch his attack on the United States by swarming the fort in the Straits.

Thus began the War of 1812. Although, for 21st-century Americans, it does not evoke the patriotic zeal of either the Revolutionary War or the Civil War, it was a very important and controversial period in U.S. history. Unlike the Revolutionary War, the events leading to the War of 1812 deeply divided the new nation's citizens. Before the war was declared, the British leaders truly felt that the United States would soon collapse under the weight of its enormous size, unproven democratic structure and fractious leadership.

Once begun, if the war had gone Britain's way, it would be easy to imagine, from our current perspective in time, how the shaky United States government *could* have collapsed. The entire continent might easily have reverted to British control. Imagine, for a moment, what that would mean to you, your state, your country and, in fact, the world.

Remember: Politically, financially and emotionally, our country was about to dissolve into a bunch of weak, ineffectual states. Political leaders from the America's southern region openly hated the northern statesmen. The feeling of distrust was mutual. Well before the Revolutionary War, the two sections of the country bickered incessantly over the slavery issue. It was not until the two sides agreed not to disagree on this matter that they were able to join sides against their true adversary, King George III of England. Once the War for Independence was resolved (1776-1783), the old issue of slavery re-emerged, and the bickering began again in earnest.

Sadly, as always, the basis of the argument was not

so much the principle, but the money. Southern landowners could not produce their crops without cheap slave labor. Before long, the New England delegates to Congress were seriously considering seceding from the Union if the Southern delegates didn't relent on their proposal to go to war against the British.

Meanwhile, the British embargo against our ports was crippling our eastern states' economy. Our nation's treasury was bankrupt. The country was unable to repay loans to France, Holland and other countries that had lent money (often at exorbitant rates) during the Revolutionary War to defeat Britain. At the same time, if Napoleon Bonaparte's army hadn't been taking up most of England's resources in their war on the Continent (Europe), the British could have sent an enormous army to our shores and put our young government out of its misery right then.

On the other hand, if the American forces had gotten a few breaks early in the campaign (Fort Michilimackinac, for example), the United States might now include Manitoba, Quebec, Ontario and all the other Canadian provinces. Those circumstances and consequences were very real.

The *Caledonia*, the ship Captain Roberts used to attack Fort Michilimackinac, was real. The 70-ton schooner was built at Amherstberg, Ontario, in 1807. It was owned by the British-controlled North West Fur Company. In real life, as in the story, it had been in the service of the British company, taking pelts that had been brought from all over the upper lakes by the French-Canadian voyageurs in their bateaux to Michilimackinac. The *Caledonia* crew then loaded those pelts and took them east to be sold in markets all over the world. As in the story, when war was declared, General Isaac Brock requisitioned the *Caledonia* into service for the King. From this point on, the *Caledonia* followed the route to Fort St. Joseph in the St. Mary's River and into the hands of Captain Charles Roberts as described in the story. At 10 a.m. on July 16, she sailed to Michilimackinac, escorting, by one account, 42 regular British soldiers, 4 officers, 260 Canadians, 572 Chippewas and Ottawas, 56 Sioux, 48 Winnebagos and 39 Menomonees to the encounter. Also aboard were two 6-pound artillery cannon, one of which would be hauled to a point overlooking Fort Michilimackinac's north wall on July 17, 1812. After the attack, the *Caledonia* became a full-fledged part of the British naval forces.

A few months later, the *Caledonia*'s fortunes changed. Lt. Jesse Duncan Elliott of the United States Navy captured it on Oct. 8, 1812, at Fort Erie. Thereafter, the ship became a vital part of America's naval arsenal. On September 10, 1813, with the *Caledonia* in his fleet, Oliver Hazard Perry engaged the entire British naval task force in Lake Erie. The American victory there contributed to what might have been the turning point in the entire war.

How did the war end?

The Treaty of Ghent, signed on December 24, 1814, didn't become known here in Michigan Territory until the middle of the next summer. During that time, British interests retained, for as long as they could, the resources and wealth of the fur-trading center. Finally, Fort Michilimackinac was returned to United States hands on July 18, 1815, three years and a day after Lieutenant Hanks surrendered to Captain Charles Roberts on the fields behind the old fort. Mackinac Island was, as mentioned in the story, the site of both the first and the last activities in the War of 1812.

GLOSSARY

Aft: the back end of a boat

Ahoy: sailor talk for "Hi." Standard hailing cry to attract the attention of those aboard another boat

Avast: watch out or listen up! Stop what you're doing!

Aye: yes, okay, yup, uh-huh—anything in the affirmative

Barbarize: use of a soap and sand mixture to clean a surface, usually a ship's deck

Belay: to put a stop to something. On a ship, it usually means to secure a rope to a wooden pin.

Bitt the cable: attach a cable to something to hold it in place

Bitt the halyard: fasten the particular rope that keeps the halyard from going out

Boatswain (Bos'n) (Bosun): a ship's petty officer in charge of sails, rigging, etc., and summoning men to duty. Also metes out punishment, pipes orders and otherwise handles crew's discipline

Boom: the long spar, hinged at one end, that holds a sail to a mast. It is aptly named, for when the wind shifts or the boat turns, the boom flies across the deck and can easily knock an unfortunate sailor off the ship.

Bowsprit: the spar extending forward from the stem of a ship to which the stays of the foremast are fastened

Brig: the ship's jail, also in England spelled gaol (but pronounced jail)

Burgoo: boiled oatmeal porridge, seasoned with salt, sugar and butter (Orig. Norse)

Cabin boy: young male who attends to officers or passengers aboard ship

Capstan: a revolving barrel on a vertical axis for winding cable aboard ship, worked by persons walking round, pushing bars fitting into its hub

Chanteyman: a boatswain who was an experienced leader, said to be worth his weight in gold to a captain, for in the course of a long sail he would not only keep up the spirits of his crew with a large repertoire of songs, but he could pick just the right one and sing it at just the right tempo to get a particular job done without exhausting his workers

Cheerily: nautical–quickly, with haste. Also, term used to encourage work with urgency

Companion ladder: steps leading from one deck to another

Dandyfunk: broken ship's biscuits soaked with water and baked with fat and molasses

Davy Jones's Locker: domain at the bottom of the sea, the ultimate destination of drowned men and foundered ships

Deadlight: nautical—a wooden block to stop water from coming into a porthole during a storm

Deep-six: nautical expression meaning to jettison—drop overboard—get rid of something or someone

Dog watch: A day aboard a ship is divided into six 4-hour periods. The dog watch is the time between 4 p.m. and 8 p.m.

Doubloon: Spanish gold coin of double value

Dray: a horse-drawn cart with no side rails—used for hauling heavy goods and materials; still actively in use on Mackinac Island

Dreadnaught: a fearless person. Also a class of British battleship

Dried horse: dried meat of a variety of sources (beef, sheep and horse—yes, really) served to sailors aboard 19th-century ships

Forecastle (Fo'c's'le): the forward part of the upper deck. Because the bow of a sailing ship took the brunt of the water's pounding, its accommodations were less comfortable than those at the stern (where the officers stayed). In merchant ships, the seamen's quarters (also referred to as 'Before the mast') were where the laboring class of seamen resided. Fo'c's'le chanteys were "story" songs sung for fun by common seamen and not "work" songs as were sung by the chanteyman, the taskmaster of the ship, to get a particular job done.

Galley: ship's kitchen

Graveyard watch: term aboard ship for period of duty from midnight to 4 a.m.

Grog: rum diluted with water

Grub: sailors' food, which, coincidentally, was often infested with worms (grubs)

Gunwale (Gunnel or gunwhale): uppermost planking on a ship's side

Halyard: rope or tackle used to hoist or lower a sail, yard or gaff

Hard alee: or Helm's alee: warning to sailors that the ship is about to change direction and to watch one's head because the "boom" will soon follow

Haul out the watch: orders to bring off-duty crewmen up to the deck for emergency action such as bad weather, completion of voyage, or an attack by a foreign ship

Head: the ship's lavatory

Horse marine: a clumsy or awkward seaman—a person more used to riding aboard a horse than a ship

Hove to: nautical—when a ship came alongside a pier or another ship to disembark

Hundred lashes: the punishment a captain might invoke upon a sailor for breaking a ship's rules. The result frequently was fatal.

Impressed (or pressed): a seaman who is taken aboard an enemy ship to serve without his consent. The British use of these strategies upon American sailors led, in part, to the War of 1812.

Jay Treaty: settlement in 1795 between the U.S. and Britain, which ceded vast tracts of territory to the U.S. This was very unpopular among British fur-trading interests. Said to lay the groundwork for the War of 1812

Keel haul: Punishment in which an accused sailor was tied to a rope and thrown overboard. He was drawn, by another rope, under the keel, from one side of the ship to the other. This punishment was often fatal. Survival depended on the sailor's offense—and the feelings of the ship's officers, who, as they pulled the ropes, could either save the offending sailor by hauling him swiftly beneath the ship's hull or, by drawing him slowly, cause the victim to drown. Such was the fate, life or death, of many 19th-century sailors.

Landlubber: lazy or clumsy seaman; one without sufficient experience or skill to properly sail or operate a ship

Lashes: short for "hundred lashes," which was the maximum number of whips dealt as penalty aboard ship. "You'll get your lashes for this, sure you will!" That was a common threat aboard any merchant ship and sure to strike fear into the heart of any sailor. The wounds from "a hundred lashes" would surely be fatal.

Lime juice: obligatory ration aboard British ships to combat scurvy

Limey: British sailor

List: ship tilting to one side due to flooding or cargo shift

Lobscouse: stew consisting of salt meat, potatoes, hardtack, onions and available spices

Manito: also Manedo and Manitou: Indian spirit. Gitchimanitou and Kitchimanedo (other attempted phonetic spellings apply) is the Great Spirit, the Supreme Being

Man-o'-war: class of British battleship

Master: officer in command of a merchant ship

Mate: First mate is second in command of ship, below Master.

Mess room: area where ship's company would take their meals

Monkey: nautical expression for a small size of something, such as a jacket. There is also a monkey shift, for example, which is a short time on deck.

Mooring ball: floating device anchored offshore to tie a boat when not in use

Morning watch: the time aboard ship between 4 a.m. and 8 a.m.

Nee-mush: Native American term for milkweed pod, used in stews and soups

Pieces of eight: coins that could be cut into halves, quarters and eighths and used to make change. Each part would be a bit, hence the expression, "Shave and a haircut, two bits"—two bits equaling 25 cents.

Pinch: to steal; something that has been stolen

Pin-ik: Native American term for wild potato

Poor Jack: fish salted and dried for eating aboard ship

Port: left-hand side of ship as viewed from the stern

Porthole: circular opening in a vessel's sides to admit ventilation and light

Privateer: literally a private individual not under orders from any one nation. He does his country a service by stealing an enemy country's resources; in this case, its ships, their men and cargo. A privateer, or pirate, keeps all that he gets for himself.

Quarterdeck: the upper deck from the mainmast back to the ship's stern

Rudder: hinged device at the stern of a vessel by which she is steered

Running downward, weather helm: a ship moving with full wind behind it; like a runaway freight train—unstoppable

Sail close to the wind: dangerous stupidity; to take a chance, especially with authority or accepted ship standards. The term comes from the peril, nautically, of the situation where, should the wind shift, the sails could snap their lines and the ship would founder. Figuratively, it is a person who goes off on his own without heeding common sense.

Salt: an experienced sailor

Scurvy: a disease caused by lack of vitamin C often seen aboard ships due to long voyages without fresh fruits, especially citrus

Slops: clothing kept in the ship's chest—a store owned by the master of the ship (captain) and operated by an assistant—for sailors who came aboard without proper apparel—often because of being pressed against their will into service

Stanchion: a vertical post supporting a ship's guard railing

Starboard: right-hand side of ship as viewed from the stern

Stem to stern: from front to back; the whole ship

Stone: an English measure of weight equal to 14 pounds

Tack: the direction a ship is traveling, often dictated by the wind or sea conditions

Thwart: a transverse beam on a rowboat, providing structural stability as well as a bench for the rowers or passengers to sit on

Vittles: slang for victuals, supplies of food

Zush-ka-boo-bish: Native American dish made from muskrat, skinned, cut into small pieces, then roasted until brown and boiled until tender, then put in a pot with pin-ik and nee-mush

BIBLIOGRAPHY

Michael Dousman, Term Paper by Margaret Doud
CMU 1965

Historic Mackinac, two volumes,
Edwin O. Wood 1918

Lake Huron, Fred Landon 1944

Michigan, Willis F. Dunbar 1965

Les Cheneaux Chronicles, Philip Pittman 1984

The British Army at Mackinac, Brian Leigh
Dunnigan 1980

War of 1812, George May 1962

About the Author:

Robert Lytle, a pharmacist and drugstore owner for over 30 years, took up writing as a hobby only fifteen years ago. Since then, he has had seven books published. The five Mackinac Passage stories loosely describe his childhood summers in Michigan's upper peninsula. The two others depict early Michigan life as witnessed through the eyes of two young, modern-day time travelers.

A Saginaw, Michigan native, Bob summered in upper Michigan's resort community of the Les Cheneaux Islands. He then worked at various jobs on Mackinac Island while studying pharmacy at Ferris State.

After graduation, Bob and his wife raised their four sons in Rochester where they bought and renovated a hundred-year-old pharmacy on Main Street. It was while researching the history of that building that he became interested in Michigan's past. What he learned prompted him to write two time-travel adventures, *Three Rivers Crossing* and *A Pitch In Time*, both of which are being used extensively in Michigan Schools.

Still active in his pharmacy, Bob enjoys breaking away to visit schools. His presentations range from reading poems to second-grade classes to sharing publishing secrets with college-age English majors.

About the Illustrator:

Pirate Party is the second book illustrated by Bill Williams for Robert Lytle. The first book was the award winning, *A Pitch In Time*. Bill's art can be found in corporate, museum and private collections throughout the U.S. His ability to create art in oil, pastel, charcoal and graphite has made him a popular artist with college and professional sports teams, celebrities and art publishers. Bill's paintings are part of the permanent collection in Cooperstown's Baseball Hall of Fame and the College Football Hall of Fame. He has received numerous awards for his art. Bill and his wife, Sharon, live in Battle Creek. They have two sons. Bill Williams' art can be seen at www.billwilliamsart.com and www.goodsportsart.com.

Other Books By Robert A. Lytle

Mackinac Passage: A Summer Adventure

Fifteen-year-old Pete Jenkins meets two boys and a girl near his summer cabin in northern Michigan. The new friends find clues linking a hermit writer to a counterfeit money scheme. Setting aside other activities for the intrigue of spying, they follow the elderly man by sail to nearby Mackinac Island. To their horror, the tale turns to one of murder. A test of wills leads them through a series of terrifying obstacles to a remarkable conclusion. 178 pages

Mackinac Passage: The Boathouse Mystery

Fifteen-year-old Pete Jenkins and his three summer friends return to their cottages following a perilous escapade on nearby Mackinac Island. They soon learn that many boathouses in the Les Cheneaux Islands resort community are being looted - theirs included. Curiosity prevails and the teens investigate. Unknown to them, however, the escaped Mackinac murderer lurks in the shadows plotting a fiendish scheme of revenge. 176 pages

Mackinac Passage: The General's Treasure

As a reward for their heroics, fifteen-year-old Pete Jenkins and his three Cincinnati Row friends revisit the Andersons at their magnificent cottage on Mackinac Island. Pete's idea of rest and relaxation is soon interrupted by a chance meeting with an elderly heiress. She presents Pete with a seemingly worthless poem which leads the inquisitive teens to various sites around the Island - and ultimately into the perilous grasp of a deranged treasure hunter. 172 pages

Three Rivers Crossing

Walker Morrison, a modern-day, thirteen-year-old boy, goes fly-fishing near his home in Rochester, Michigan. Suddenly trapped underwater, he awakens to find himself on the bank of the river 180 years in the past, rescued by his own great-great-great-great grandfather. Walker reveals his secret to another boy, Daniel Taylor, his great-great-great-granduncle, and together they work to return Walker to his own time. In the meantime, he learns to adapt to living on the frontier in the 1820s with his new family. 161 pages

Mackinac Passage: Mystery At Round Island Light

The 4th book in Robert Lytle's Mackinac Island Mystery Series ... Pete Jenkins and his three friends are spending the summer on beautiful Mackinac Island. Join the adventure as they explore a suppose-to-be haunted lighthouse and find more than just ghosts! 151 pages

A Pitch In Time

Tells the tale of a modern day boy who tumbles from his bike and wakes up to find he has traveled back in time to the spring of 1864 in rural Michigan during the Civil War. His southern accent, cultural views and even the sport he loves all come in conflict with everything he has ever known. The story unfolds as his new 19th century friend, Sally Norton, helps him learn the ways of a war-torn Northern community. 316 pages

To order, call EDCO at 888-510-3326
or visit us at www.edcopublishing.com

2648 Lapeer Rd
Auburn Hills, MI 48326

YES!
I want to read other exciting books written by Robert Lytle

Mackinac Passage: A Summer Adventure	$12.95
Mackinac Passage: The Boathouse Mystery	$ 8.95
Mackinac Passage: The General's Treasure	$12.95
Mystery at Round Island Light (Hardcover)	$15.95
Mystery at Round Island Light (Softcover)	$ 8.95
Three Rivers Crossing	$ 8.95
Three Rivers Crossing (Teachers Guide)	$ 3.50
A Pitch In Time	$12.95
A Pitch In Time CONNECT-IT™	$29.95

To order, call EDCO at 888-510-3326 or visit us at www.edcopublishing.com

*Prices subject to change without notice